WIKILEAKS
AND THE AGE OF
TRANSPARENCY

WIKILEAKS AND THE AGE OF TRANSPARENCY

Micah L. Sifry

COUNTERPOINT | BERKELEY

Library of Congress Cataloging-in-Publication Data is available.

ISBN 978-1-58243-779-8

Printed in the United States of America

COUNTERPOINT
1919 Fifth Street
Berkeley, CA 94710

www.counterpointpress.com

Distributed by Publishers Group West

10 9 8 7 6 5 4 3 2 1

TABLE OF CONTENTS

To my parents Anna and Benny
who taught me that the truth matters

WIKILEAKS
AND THE AGE OF
TRANSPARENCY

FOREWORD

Andrew Rasiej

In 2008, my then eighty-two-year-old father received a call from a Polish military historian who had uncovered an old file secretly hidden for sixty-seven years. It contained a list with the names of Polish prisoners of war who had been killed in the basement of the headquarters of the Soviet secret police in Kiev in 1940 on the orders of Josef Stalin. Until this file was discovered, these men were part of a missing group of 7,000 out of a total of 22,000 POWs, mostly officers, who were murdered in what is known as the Katyn Massacre.

Among those 7,000 names was my father's father, Zigmunt Rasiej. My grandfather was the county police commissioner in the town of Brody in the eastern part of Poland when he was arrested, imprisoned, then executed and buried in an unmarked mass grave just outside Kiev. Until 1992, Russian authorities had claimed that the Nazis killed these 22,000 men as they retreated from Moscow in the winter of 1943.

In 1940, had a fair-minded Soviet soldier came across

secret Politburo documents indicating that the Poles were to be systematically murdered, had this same person leaked those documents to media throughout the free world—whatever might have befallen that whistleblower, the fate of those men—the intellectual elite, the leaders of Polish society—would have certainly been different. The result might even have altered the course of the war. Who knows? I do believe that if such information had been leaked, my grandfather would not have died with a bullet to the back of his head along with his fellow countrymen.

History is rife with examples of people suffering the consequences of duplicity and hypocrisy by government and institutional leaders. My family's story about persecution at the hands of unjust individuals is not unique: it is still being repeated on a daily basis around the world—thousands of times.

I am watching with fascination as the WikiLeaks saga unfolds. I have tried my best to separate my feelings about its embattled founder, Julian Assange, from the greater questions that now need answers. What is the nature of information in a connected age? Does the Internet and technology help or hurt the cause of free speech and human rights? Can companies like Amazon, Paypal, Google, Twitter, Facebook, Mastercard, etc. at once aim for a profit, exploit the advantages of the Internet, and behave morally? How can we ensure that whistleblowers continue to speak out when needed? And is WikiLeaks a symptom of decades of governmental and institutional opacity, or is it a disease that needs to be stopped at all costs?

These questions, and the debates over the answers, will continue to rage long after this book gets downloaded for the last time. But we have clearly entered a new chapter in human history, where information technology has advanced so far as to render law, regulation, and social conventions powerless to keep up with its ability to change the course of human events.

Where do we go from here?

Governments, like people, need to keep some secrets, withholding information from time to time, to achieve reasonable goals. Discretion is part of the social fabric binding people in their personal lives and in business. It is reasonable to allow diplomats, military planners, and even politicians the freedom to use secrets in the service of their country.

However, there is a difference between withholding information and blatantly lying to the people to whom one is accountable. The issue is not whether WikiLeaks did the right thing, or whether it should even exist. The real question is what responsibility do governments and institutions like them (for example, the Roman Catholic Church) have to build systems within their power structures so that they remain accountable? When those in power work harder to protect themselves than they do to maintain mechanisms of oversight and justice, opacity wins out over transparency—but only for a limited time. Eventually, a weak link in the hierarchy of power shows up. What is needed is not a call for radical transparency, which some might interpret WikiLeaks' mission to be. Rather, we should be demanding that the default setting for institutional power be "open," and when needed those same powers should be forced to argue when things need to remain closed. Right now, the default setting is "closed," and the public is just left arguing.

Laws and regulations must be updated to reflect that freedom of speech in our connected, networked, and handheld printing press world is different from what our forefathers imagined when including it at the heart of the Constitution. The hypocrisy of the American government's reaction to WikiLeaks is a case in point. If we promote the use of the Internet to overturn repressive regimes around the world, then we have to either accept the fact that these same methods may be used against our own regime—or make sure our own policies are beyond reproach.

The people and companies behind the technology need to be transparent about what information they collect. They need to develop consistent policies to allow individuals to opt in, or out, of their data collection systems. They also need to develop standards so that people quickly learn of government requests for their documentation or information about them. We must have a right to protect the privacy of information stored in the cloud as rigorously as if it were in our own home. Finally, there must be widespread acknowledgment that much of our public discourse occurs on corporate networks and servers, and these corporations must robustly defend the open Internet that they are so handily profiting from. Angry rhetoric from politicians or a hint of a possible criminal investigation should not be enough to cause companies to kick unpopular speakers off their services.

Lastly, citizens must educate themselves. Each time we buy a new gadget from Apple or sign up for another two-year contract from Verizon, post a photo on Facebook, or drive through a tollbooth, we join a never-ending dance of data collection with not a clue as to what the consequences might be. There are those who argue that such collection of data about every click, every download, or transit card swipe make our lives more convenient, efficient, and safer, and in many ways they are right. But what price do we pay? What will we do when the net becomes so powerful we can't escape it, that we can't find even a semblance of privacy or not be able to define it for ourselves any longer?

As you read my colleague and friend Micah Sifry's thorough analysis of the WikiLeaks phenomenon and how it fits into the much larger global movement for transparency, I hope we can agree that a future where citizens are the ultimate authority requires the best, most timely, and most accurate information. Interestingly, that's the same reason Julian Assange says he created WikiLeaks in the first place.

INTRODUCTION

All governments lie, but disaster lies in wait for countries whose officials smoke the same hashish they give out.

— I. F. Stone

This book is not a treatise on WikiLeaks, nor is it meant to be an exhaustive discussion of the future of secrecy or privacy, or a comprehensive exploration of all the ways the Internet is changing politics, governance, and society. It has been, however, called into existence by WikiLeaks and the urgent debates that have been ignited by the actions of its founder Julian Assange and his supporters around the world. But readers should be forewarned—I am not aiming to untangle every knotty question raised by WikiLeaks, nor do I think it would be wise to try, given how quickly that story continues to develop and change. But with the current volley of books appearing about Assange, WikiLeaks, and the ins-and-outs of his relations with various major news organizations, there's a danger of missing the bigger story of what WikiLeaks really represents.

I have conceived of this book as a report from the trenches where a wide array of small-d democracy and transparency activists are hard at work using new tools and methods to open up powerful institutions and make them more accountable, and to situate WikiLeaks in that movement. For some of these activists, this little book will likely cover mostly familiar ground. For others, it may be helpful in connecting the dots of what is happening to better see how the pieces fit together. But my real goal in writing it is to explain to others what I think is going on, and perhaps convince them that it is time to join in.

An old way of doing things is dying; a new one is being born. And we need more midwives.

What is new is our ability to individually and together connect with greater ease than at any time in human history. As a result, information flows more freely into the public arena, powered by seemingly unstoppable networks of people around the world cooperating to share vital data and prevent its suppression. Old institutions and incumbent powers are inexorably coming to terms with this new reality. The "Age of Transparency" is here: not because one transnational online network dedicated to open information and whistle-blowing named WikiLeaks exists, but because the knowledge of how to build and maintain such networks is now widespread.

It both helps and hurts that we are living in a time of radical uncertainty about the "official" version of the truth. All kinds of "authoritative" claims made by leading public figures in recent years have turned out to be little more than thin air. There were no weapons of mass destruction in Iraq. Deregulation of Wall Street didn't make the financial marketplace more rational. The American housing market turned out to be built on sand. The extent of Federal Reserve subsidies to the financial sector during the 2008–09 market collapse turned out to be much larger than was originally disclosed. The dikes of New Orleans weren't built to withstand a major hurricane. The Catholic Church child-molestation scandals turned out to be more widespread than church officials claimed. The oil wells in the Gulf weren't safe as promised and ratified by government inspectors. (And the claim that no one imagined that any of these things could go wrong and no one tried to warn us in advance? Also false.) Even on smaller issues, the "authorities" often turn out to be the last to know what is actually going on, especially now that we all use the real-time web to share what we know as events unfold. Nothing less than absolute transparency for powerful actors seems to be the remedy to this state of affairs, the only way to restore trust in public institutions. And yet we also know we cannot eliminate all secrets nor live in a world where privacy and confidentiality no longer exist.

In 2004, along with Andrew Rasiej, I helped found Personal Democracy Forum. Together with Andrew's and my work with the Sunlight Foundation, which we helped start in 2006, I have had a front row seat as an observer, and sometimes a place on stage as a participant, as this drama of network-powered politics plays out. This book is informed by those experiences. At times it is written in the first person, because I was a witness to, or participant in, the events described. But it is also in the first person because I think that is the only honest voice I can use. This is a subjective, biased view of how the great clash between power, authority, truth, data, access, participation, and democracy is unfolding in our newly networked age. I don't believe anyone can have a totally objective view of history, and certainly not from this close to the trenches. People who claim otherwise come from what I consider to be an outdated and untenable world of journalism that never made much sense, and certainly can't make sense in an age when we are all direct observers and potential participants in the telling of the story of our time. But I trust that by sharing my personal viewpoints, you the reader can make a better judgment of what you are reading about, and how my biases may color the picture.

Since this book is inspired by the WikiLeaks controversy, I will start by sharing some of what I have come to know of its founder through the course of my work, while reviewing the highlights of WikiLeaks' last year. But then I will take a turn back to the early years of this century, when the World Wide Web was just starting to become politically relevant, before YouTube, Facebook, and Twitter, when the main tools for building transparent and connected communities were blogs, email lists and live conversation tools like Internet Relay Chat. In my humble opinion, that is when things really began to change. I will then explore the rise of the transparency movement in the United States, as well as its counterparts in countries around the world. And I will look at how authorities are responding, in some cases by opening up to the new energies of civic participation but in most cases falling short by choosing to avoid or withdraw from public conversation and engagement. Finally, I will come back to the current fight over WikiLeaks' activities and what it shows about the potential and limits of Internet freedom.

WikiLeaks is just one piece of a much larger continuum of changes in how the people and the powerful relate to each other in this new time—changes that are fundamentally healthy for the growth and strength of an open society. Secrecy and the hoarding of information are ending; openness and the sharing of information are coming.

As I write these words, we seem to have reached a hinge moment in that cleansing process which now stretches from the once-secret ledgers of the Federal Reserve and the not-so-hidden dealings of the U.S. State Department to the streets of the Middle East and North Africa. America's leaders, some of them advocates for greater transparency in government at home and abroad, seem shocked that an outside force is doing to them what they have long called on democracy activists in other countries to do to their governments. Other political figures haven't even tried to balance open government with their knee-jerk attacks on WikiLeaks and calls for Assange's imprisonment or assassination. Dangerous legal precedents may soon be created that undermine the long-standing freedom of the press to report the truth.

American technology companies seem mostly cowed by the furious blasts emanating from Washington and uncertain of their own commitment to defend free speech online. While some tech visionaries are speaking out, others have been disturbingly quiet about the willingness of large chunks of their industry to cave in so quickly to political pressure. And American democracy activists seem divided between those who want to fight with extralegal methods to defend the wide-open web, those who fear engendering an anti-WikiLeaks backlash (or distrust Assange personally and fear being tied to his mast), and those like me who are resolutely anti-anti-WikiLeaks, and worry that the "cure" to WikiLeaks' independence will be worse than the disease.

While it is impossible to predict which way things will go, I hope this book can serve as a guide to help better understand how we got here, and thus also a resource for charting a sensible way forward.

—Micah L. Sifry
New York, January 2011

1

The WikiLeaks Moment

Every time we witness an act that we feel to be unjust and do not act we become a party to injustice. Those who are repeatedly passive in the face of injustice soon find their character corroded into servility. Most witnessed acts of injustice are associated with bad governance, since when governance is good, unanswered injustice is rare. By the progressive diminution of a people's character, the impact of reported but unanswered injustice is far greater than it may initially seem. Modern communications states through their scale, homogeneity, and excesses provide their populace with an unprecedented deluge of witnessed, but seemingly unanswerable injustices.

— Julian Assange,
"Conspiracy as Governance," December 3, 2006

Back in the fall of 2009, getting hold of Julian Assange wasn't easy. The Australian founder of WikiLeaks seemed to be constantly on the move, and his email habits were unpredictable. Andrew Rasiej and I had invited him to speak at the inaugural European gathering of the Personal Democracy

Forum (PdF) in Barcelona that November. "Micah, great!" he wrote in late October, accepting the invitation. "Currently in Laos. Denmark 18th Nov-ish. Iceland not long after. Can you send me all necessary details?"

I wrote back right away, but a series of follow-up emails to his Sunshinepress.org account failed to get a response. The conference was just a few weeks away and we weren't sure if one of our keynote speakers was really coming. In desperation, I went online to the WikiLeaks.org website and clicked on "live chat." Within moments another screen opened, and I was given an anonymous user account name. I typed hello, and someone responded, telling me his name was "Daniel." I started to explain who I was, and Daniel suggested opening a private one-on-one chat to continue the conversation. No, Julian wasn't available right now, he told me, but he promised to relay my messages to him.

He did, because two weeks later, Assange and his trusted colleague Daniel (who then went by the pseudonym Daniel Schmitt, but has since broken with WikiLeaks and is now known by his real name, Daniel Domscheit-Berg) were with us at the hypermodern Torre Agbar building in Barcelona, where some 350 people from all over Europe had come to PdF to talk about how technology was changing politics. The speakers included the top online organizers of the Barack Obama presidential campaign of 2008; senior tech advisers to the English, French, Spanish, German, and Norwegian governments; leaders from companies like Google, Facebook, and Meetup; and a polyglot mix of political bloggers, social media consultants, e-democracy innovators, human rights activists, and transparency advocates. But everyone seemed slightly awed by Assange and Domscheit-Berg, who were already known then among the digerati for what they had achieved with WikiLeaks.

Since its founding in late 2006, the nonprofit online media organization had published hundreds of exposés and critical documents, including more than 6,500 Congressional Research Service reports, most of which were previously only available to members of Congress and their staffs; proof of high-level government corruption and human rights abuses in Kenya; confidential records of one of Iceland's top banks revealing its role in the country's financial collapse; details on the hyper-secretive Church of Scientology's operations; and a Guantánamo Bay prison procedures manual that the American Civil Liberties Union had been unable to obtain under the Freedom of Information Act. Amnesty International gave WikiLeaks an award for its reporting on Kenya, and the British organization Index on Censorship honored it for having stared down the Swiss bank Julian Bär, which had obtained an injunction shutting down its main web domain. That act had boomeranged against the bank, as WikiLeaks supporters around the world swiftly set up mirror sites to keep it in public view.

Earlier that month, WikiLeaks had struck another blow for freedom of information. The night of Monday, October 12, the website of the English newspaper *The Guardian* posted a strange article saying that it was being stopped from reporting on a question pending in Parliament. "*The Guardian* is prevented from identifying the MP who has asked the question, what the question is, which minister might answer it, or where the question is to be found," the paper's David Leigh wrote. "*The Guardian* is also forbidden from telling its readers why the paper is prevented—for the first time in memory—from reporting parliament. Legal obstacles, which cannot be identified, involve proceedings, which cannot be mentioned, on behalf of a client who must remain secret."[1]

The only thing *The Guardian* could say was that the case involved Carter-Ruck, a prominent legal firm that specializes in working with global corporations. The British blogosphere went into overdrive speculating about the case, and swiftly zeroed in on a report,[2] posted to WikiLeaks,[3] connecting the oil commodity firm Trafigura to toxic dumping off the coast of Africa. Apparently Carter-Ruck was trying to keep the issue from surfacing publicly and had obtained a court injunction barring coverage of a pending question that was being raised on the matter by a member of Parliament. The word "Trafigura" also took off on Twitter, making Carter-Ruck's legal efforts essentially moot. It was a textbook example of WikiLeaks at its most powerful, preventing the suppression of information that everyone agreed deserved to be aired in public.

On stage in Barcelona for the final plenary at the forum, Assange didn't talk much about how the Internet and new communications technologies made WikiLeaks' work possible. Instead, he called on Western journalists and transparency activists to do more to keep governments and business honest.

"A friend of mine in the United States, Daniel Ellsberg, who famously leaked the Pentagon Papers, uses a phrase that I've become fond of," he said, leaning into the microphone for emphasis. "'Courage is contagious,' that is, when someone engages in a courageous act and shows other people that that act wasn't an act of martyrdom, rather that it was an intelligently designed act, it encourages other people to follow him."

Assange went on to argue that such courage was needed not just in the developing world, but also in the advanced countries of Europe, using words that in retrospect seem eerily prophetic.

> Why aren't more journalists being arrested in Europe? Why aren't more transparency activists being arrested in Europe? It's not because Europe has no problems. It's not because Europe is a gentle society .... Europe is involved in big geopolitical games internally, it's overrun with Russian oligarchs, there are extreme problems in Europe .... Where is the civil courage amongst civil society in Europe? I see some of it, but I think there should be more .... I encourage you to not become martyrs, but instead to intelligently

understand how far you can push government into doing something that is just, by exposing injustice.[4]

By the spring of 2010, it was becoming clear that Assange wasn't only thinking about exposing injustice in Europe, but was also growing more focused on the United States government. In January, WikiLeaks' Twitter account made a curious call for help: "Have encrypted videos of U.S. bomb strikes on civilians. We need super computer time."[5] Then in April came an explosive video, published by WikiLeaks on a free-standing site, CollateralMurder.com. This was a decrypted military video showing two U.S. Apache helicopter gunships firing on and killing about a dozen Iraqi civilians, including two employees of Reuters, on July 12, 2007. Assange flew to Washington from Reykjavik to present the video at a widely attended press conference at the National Press Club, but this was to be his last visit to the United States, for reasons that were soon to become clear.

Introducing the video, Assange informed the audience that the Pentagon had told Reuters the killings had not violated the military's rules of engagement. "I believe that if those killings were lawful under the rules of engagement, then the rules of engagement are wrong," he declared. "The behavior of the pilots is like they're playing a video game. Their desire is to get high scores in their computer game."[6]

The "Collateral Murder" video drove worldwide attention to WikiLeaks and its founder. Soon, Assange was on a full-fledged media tour, complete with a stop on Comedy Central's *Colbert Report*, where host Stephen Colbert jokingly accused him of "trying to bum us out about the world." To laughter from both Assange and the audience, Colbert added, "If we don't know what the government is doing, we can't be sad about it."[7] Within two weeks, the seventeen-minute YouTube version of the helicopter video had been viewed six million times—a huge audience for such a long piece of online content.

"Collateral Murder" also marked a bit of a departure for Assange and WikiLeaks, in that the organization decided to put a strong editorial stamp on the material, rather than simply post it online and let other news organizations put it into context. A team of volunteers worked for weeks on preparing the video and accompanying material, and some even traveled to Iraq to track down relatives of the airstrike's victims.[8] "The promise we make to our sources," Assange explained to Colbert, "is that not only will we defend through every means that we have available, but we will try to get the maximum possible political impact for the material they give to us."[9] The video also fueled a big boost in WikiLeaks' fortunes; after having gone dark for a brief period in late 2009 to raise money, suddenly the donations were flowing in. The site's Twitter feed tweaked the mainstream media: "Raised >$150K in donations since Mon. New funding model for journalism: try doing it for a change."[10]

WikiLeaks new level of visibility prompted *New York Times* reporter Noam Cohen to pose a fascinating question: "What Would Daniel Ellsberg do with the Pentagon Papers today?" Would he have given them to *The New York Times* and waited for them to be analyzed and published? Or would he just post them online? Back in 1970–71, it had taken Ellsberg, then a high-level analyst with the Rand Corporation, several months to photocopy the ten-thousand-page secret history of America's war, and months more of efforts to get them published. Ellsberg told Cohen, "As of today, I wouldn't have waited that long. I would have gotten a scanner and put them on the Internet."

Ellsberg admitted that the government's effort to stop their publication was useful in garnering public attention; when Nixon's Justice Department got a court injunction stopping the *Times* from continuing to publish the papers, Ellsberg passed copies to *The Washington Post*. When the *Post* was enjoined from publishing, he gave them to *The Boston Globe* and *The St. Louis Post-Dispatch*, which were also then enjoined. Ultimately twenty different newspapers were publishing parts of the Pentagon Papers, even though the White House was publicly insisting their actions were irreparably harming national security. The legal battle kept the story hot until the Supreme Court ruled, by a 6-to-3 vote, against the government's efforts at censorship.

But Ellsberg was impressed by the power of the Internet to spread information beyond anyone's control. As Cohen wrote:

> Today, [Ellsberg] says, there is something enticing about being independent—not at the whim of publishers or government attempts to control release. "The government wouldn't have been tempted to enjoin it, if I had put it all out at once," he said. "We got this duel going between newspapers and the government."
>
> He does concede that something might have been lost had Wikileaks been around in 1971. "I don't think it would have had the same impact, then or now, as having it in the *Times*," he said. The government's attempt to block publication—something ended by the Supreme Court—was the best publicity, he said.
>
> But playing the government off newspapers, and newspapers against each other, still does not compare with the power of the World Wide Web. "Competition worked in a useful way," he said. "But the Internet has this viral aspect. It gets sent around and gets a broader audience."

Ellsberg admitted to Cohen that until the release of the "Collateral Murder" video he had been skeptical of WikiLeaks, noting that earlier the organization had tried to recruit him as an adviser but he had declined because he thought the site could not realistically protect would-be leakers from being discovered by government spy agencies. "I didn't believe the technology could keep them away," he told Cohen. "But the anger of the government over this leak suggests that they have been successful so far."[11]

Reading Cohen's article in the *Times*, PdF cofounder Andrew Rasiej called me and suggested we try to get Assange and Ellsberg together on stage at our June 2010 conference. It would be the first time the two had ever physically met, and a chance to explore and compare the power of Internet-driven transparency to its precursor. I sent Ellsberg the following email:

> Dan:
>
> I am writing to see if you would be interested in speaking at Personal Democracy Forum, the country's largest annual conference on how technology is changing politics. Every year we gather close to a thousand activists, journalists, bloggers, public officials, hacks, and hackers, all united in their interest in how politics and governance are being transformed by new interactive technologies. Given that we're in NY, we also devote significant time to how the media system is changing. While we are a crosspartisan event that brings together people of all political stripes, we do have one bias: we're interested in highlighting people and projects that are using technology to make the process more open, participatory, and accountable.
>
> To that end, we were fascinated by your recent comment that you would have scanned the Pentagon Papers and put them on the Internet, had the Internet existed back in the 1960s.
>
> We would like to propose a keynote session on whistle-blowing and muckraking, then and now. To keep it simple, we'd frame it as a conversation with you and Julian Assange, the cofounder of Wikileaks, who is already planning to attend . . . .

I also added a personal note, because I knew the odds of getting the seventy-nine-year-old Ellsberg on short notice to come from California to New York weren't promising:

> P.S. I have to share a personal connection between us. One of my longtime colleagues and friends is Randy Kehler, who I got to know when he was helping running the Nuclear Freeze movement and I was a young reporter at *The Nation* magazine. I heard from him the story of how you happened to hear him speak at Haverford about his preparing to go to prison to resist the war, and how that helped inspire you to leak the papers. That story has always reminded me how you never know how one person's action can change the world.
>
> A much smaller version of a tale involving Randy and *The Nation* that he told me: the Nuclear Freeze movement was a small project that he and Randall Forsberg were trying to launch using town meetings across Massachusetts back in 1980. When Reagan won in a landslide, a *Nation* intern wrote the only news story by anyone noting that nuclear freeze referenda won even LARGER vote margins in towns across western Mass—including many places where Reagan had won a majority of the vote. That little *Nation* editorial was read by two California activists, Nick and Jo Seidita, who contacted Randy and the rest is history. [They went on to fund the first statewide freeze initiative in California, which passed in 1981 and fostered a national movement that culminated with a million-strong demonstration in New York City's Central Park in June 1982.]
>
> These stories—yours and Randy's—never fail to inspire me. Even if you can't come to PdF, thank you for this opportunity to connect with you directly and share my gratitude for your life's work.

At first, Ellsberg wrote back apologizing for having to miss our conference, as he had a scheduling conflict. But a few minutes later he changed his mind, noting my mention of our mutual friend Randy Kehler. "That meeting in Haverford changed my life," he wrote. (Later, Ellsberg told me that hearing Randy's talk had struck "like a cleaver to my brain, with my past life on one side and my future on the other." In his memoir, Ellsberg writes, "What I had just heard from Randy had put the question in my mind, What could I do, what should I be doing, to help end the war now that I was ready to go to prison for it?")[12]

Quickly, Andrew wrote Assange a note: "Julian: We just confirmed Daniel Ellsberg who is coming to speak but mostly because he wants to meet you. He is not so young anymore and is traveling back and forth from CA over a 24 hour period to do this, so please confirm your availability on June 3 as soon as you know." This time Assange was quick to reply. "This was a clever enticement to be sure . . . :) I'm game."

Soon, we put out word that the June 3-4 meeting of PdF would feature a historic encounter of the two men, one who had been called "the most dangerous man in America" by then–National Security Advisor Henry Kissinger, and the other who was rapidly earning a similar reputation worldwide, by using the Internet in a radical new way. Unfortunately for our plans, bigger things were in motion.

On June 1, Assange wrote us to say that he couldn't come to New York for his PdF talk with Ellsberg two days later. "I have received urgent advice that it is unsafe for me to travel to the U.S. and am cancelling all my plans there. . . . I am not happy, but this is what happens when a country stops following the rule of law. Sorry I don't have more notice. . . ." Something had changed. After all, Assange had been in the United States just weeks earlier for the Collateral Murder press tour. But now he was not willing to risk another visit.

We ended up conducting a virtual meeting on the PdF stage in New York, with Ellsberg seated next to me and Assange plugged in via Skype video from Australia, his head projected above us like some kind of strange Big Brother image. We had some trouble with the connection, which made our dialogue somewhat stilted. But one back-and-forth with Assange stands out. I had asked him if he thought the current crackdown on whistle-blowers in the United States, where several cases are under way for what is a very rarely prosecuted crime, might be related to the existence of WikiLeaks.

He answered, "I'm not sure it's us. All our sources have not been exposed. Certainly none have been publicly exposed." (Given the timing of Assange's remarks, his careful clarification suggests he knew something might be up with his biggest source.) Having said that, he made a pitch for more sources to come forward. "Remember, almost no one gets caught. We're talking about five prosecutions in a country of three hundred million. Almost everyone who leaks material is successful. . . . It's much safer than walking across the street."

And yet, Assange would not travel to America. It is

probably not a coincidence that right around this time, at the end of May, Private Bradley Manning was arrested at his U.S. Army base east of Baghdad, on suspicion of having given classified military documents and videos, along with hundreds of thousands of secret State Department cables, to WikiLeaks. According to Wired.com, which broke the news, the authorities learned of Manning's alleged activities from a former computer hacker named Adrian Lamo, who Manning spoke to online. Lamo gave *Wired* a copy of their chat transcripts, in which Manning described leaking the Apache video, as well as a classified Army counterintelligence study evaluating WikiLeaks as a security threat, which the site had posted in March 2010.[13] He also said he had leaked 260,000 diplomatic cables that he claimed exposed "almost criminal political back dealings."

"Hillary Clinton, and several thousand diplomats around the world are going to have a heart attack when they wake up one morning, and find an entire repository of classified foreign policy is available, in searchable format, to the public," Manning reportedly wrote Lamo. "Everywhere there's a U.S. post, there's a diplomatic scandal that will be revealed," Manning wrote. "It's open diplomacy. World-wide anarchy in CSV format. It's Climategate with a global scope, and breathtaking depth. It's beautiful, and horrifying." The recipient of these leaks, Manning told Lamo at one point in the transcript: "a crazy white haired aussie who can't seem to stay in one country very long." Later he made it explicit: "Crazy white haired dude = Julian Assange."[14] (Despite this apparent statement, as of late January 2011 government investigators had reportedly not yet found a way to connect Manning directly to Assange.)[15]

Why did Manning allegedly do it? According to his dialogue with Lamo, he had been instructed to watch fifteen detainees held by the Iraqi federal police for printing "anti-Iraqi literature." Manning says he found out "they had printed a scholarly critique" against Iraqi Prime Minister Maliki, "a benign political critique titled 'Where did the money go?'... following the corruption trail within the PM's cabinet." But when Manning "*ran*" with this information to a senior officer to explain, "he didn't want to hear any of it... he told me to shut up and explain how we could assist the FPs [federal police] in finding *MORE* detainees."

After that, he said, "I saw things differently. I had always questioned the [way] things worked, and investigated to find the truth ... but that was a point where i was a *part* of something ... i was actively involved in something that i was completely against ..." Manning, it appears, knew he might be on a quixotic mission, but despite his military oath, he felt an allegiance to something higher. "Its important that it gets out... I feel, for some bizarre reason it might actually change something," he wrote Lamo. "God knows what happens now,

hopefully worldwide discussion, debates and reforms, if not . . .
then we're doomed as a species." He added, "the reaction to
the video gave me immense hope. . . . people who saw, knew
there was something wrong."

It's worth noting that, assuming the chat logs are
genuine, Manning didn't rush to leak material to Assange. He
spent some time looking at the materials he had accessed,
pondering their meaning. It took him at least six weeks
before he sent the helicopter video to WikiLeaks. At first, he
writes, it appeared to be "just a bunch of guys getting shot by
a helicopter." But he was struck by the fact that the file was
stored in a "JAG officer's directory" (Judge Advocates General,
the legal branch of the armed services), and looked further.
Gradually, he tracked down the date of the event, and then
"went to the regular internet. . . and it was still on my mind. . .
so i typed into goog. . . the date, and the location. . . and then
i see this"—a URL led him to a *New York Times* article titled,
"Two Iraqi Journalists Killed as U.S. Forces Clash With Militias."
According to the *Times*:

> The American military said in a statement late Thursday that 11
> people had been killed: nine insurgents and two civilians. According
> to the statement, American troops were conducting a raid when
> they were hit by small-arms fire and rocket-propelled grenades. The
> American troops called in reinforcements and attack helicopters. In
> the ensuing fight, the statement said, the two Reuters employees
> and nine insurgents were killed. "There is no question that
> coalition forces were clearly engaged in combat operations against

a hostile force," said Lt. Col. Scott Bleichwehl, a spokesman for the multinational forces in Baghdad.[16]

Presumably, Manning believed otherwise, as the video shows no "insurgents" being killed, just civilians. As he wrote to Lamo: "i want people to see the truth. . . regardless of who they are. . . because without information, you cannot make informed decisions as a public."[17] What started with one man's conscience offended by the suppression of information about political corruption in the Iraqi government had now expanded to a worldwide stage.

Wired's story on Manning came out on June 6. The next day, I wrote Assange to thank him for making the extra effort to keep his virtual date with Ellsberg. He responded in kind, adding, "I trust the reasons for my absence are now clear."

Over the next six months, WikiLeaks was to publish an unprecedented deluge of previously secret U.S. government documents. In July, it posted some 75,000 records of the war in Afghanistan, in coordination with *The Guardian*, *Der Spiegel*, and *The New York Times*. In October came about 400,000 documents logging the daily ups and downs of the war in Iraq. And at the end of November, WikiLeaks began publishing, again in coordination with *The Guardian*, *Der Spiegel*, *El País*, and *Le Monde* (with the *Times* brought in by *The Guardian*), a few thousand of the quarter-million confidential diplomatic cables it had obtained, presumably, from Manning.

These documents revealed that the Pentagon had lied about not keeping accurate records of the Iraqi death toll from the war and that the casualty total was perhaps 15,000 persons larger than the numbers previously made public; that U.S. authorities had failed to investigate many reports of human rights abuses by the Iraqi police and army, and had turned detainees over to the Iraqis knowing they would be tortured; that the State Department instructed American diplomats to spy on their counterparts at the United Nations; that American forces were involved in secret fighting in Yemen, which the Yemeni regime was lying to its own people about; and that the Obama administration worked closely with Republicans to protect Bush-era officials from criminal investigations in Spain regarding their possible involvement in condoning the torture of detainees.

They also exposed a wide range of previously secret actions by other countries and major corporations, including details of Pakistan's close working relationship with the Taliban, China's online assault on Google, Saudi Arabia's desire for an American attack on Iran, North Korea's support for the military dictatorship of Myanmar, Britain's role in training a Bangladeshi paramilitary group accused of being a "government death squad" by human rights monitors, and Shell Oil's deep penetration of all levels of Nigeria's government.[18] And the leaks didn't just shine light on past affairs: the release of cables from the U.S. ambassador to

Tunisia describing the country as a political kleptocracy (one was even titled, "Corruption in Tunisia: What's Yours Is Mine")[19] helped fuel a massive popular revolt against the ruling regime.

The reaction from the authorities, which I will return to later in this book, was generally hyperbolic.[20] Top officials from Vice President Joe Biden to Senate Minority Leader Mitch McConnell labeled Assange a "high-tech terrorist."[21] Secretary of State Hillary Clinton declared that the disclosures were "not just an attack on America—it's an attack on the international community," insisting he was "sabotaging the peaceful relations between nations."[22] And Senator Joe Lieberman, the chairman of the Senate committee on homeland security, started threatening companies providing services to WikiLeaks, starting with Amazon, whose resilient servers were helping keep the site online.

Within days, a host of name-brand companies, from Amazon and PayPal to Visa, MasterCard, and Bank of America, had kicked WikiLeaks off their sites, even though the group had yet to be convicted of breaking any law, much less indicted. (To their credit, Twitter and Facebook did not take similar actions.) But while WikiLeaks found safe refuge on servers based in Switzerland, along with a host of "mirror" sites put up by supporters around the world, a new phenomenon emerged. Activists affiliated with the online collective "Anonymous" organized powerful counterattacks, showering the websites of Amazon, PayPal, MasterCard, and others they perceived to be WikiLeaks' antagonists with "distributed denial-of-service" attacks, essentially paralyzing them with tens of thousands of coordinated web page requests per second. No one knew who or what was in charge of Anonymous, but we could see its members working via anonymous Internet chat rooms and collaborative writing tools.

Hailing the emergence of this resistance, the cyber-libertarian activist John Perry Barlow wrote on his Twitter feed: "The first serious infowar is now engaged. The field of battle is WikiLeaks. You are the troops."

2

The Beginning of the Age of Networked Politics

Imagine for a moment: millions of people sitting in their shuttered homes at night, bathed in that ghostly blue television aura. They're passive, yeah, but more than that: they're isolated from each other.

Now imagine another magic wire strung from house to house, hooking all these poor bastards up. They're still watching the same old crap. Then, during the touching love scene, some joker lobs an off-color aside—and everybody hears it. Whoa! What was that? People are rolling on the floor laughing. And it begins to happen so often, it gets abbreviated: ROTFL. The audience is suddenly connected to itself.

— *Christopher Locke, co-author,*
The Cluetrain Manifesto, *1999*

Infowar can mean only one thing: the conflict between the naturally open information systems of the present and the closed ones of the past. If I had to put a start date on when this process started to change politics, I'd go with April 23, 2003. It was 4:31 p.m. (EST) when Mathew Gross, then one of the first bloggers hired to work on Howard Dean's presidential campaign, posted the following on the message board of SmirkingChimp.com, an online forum for anti-Bush sentiment with about 20,000 active members:

"Ask the Dean Campaign"

So I wander back to my desk and there really IS a note on my chair from Joe Trippi, the Campaign Manager for Howard Dean. The note says:

Matt,

Start an "Ask the Dean Campaign" thread over at the Smirking Chimp.

—Joe

Surely a seminal moment in Presidential politics, no?

So, here's the deal. Use this space to throw questions and comments our way. I'll be checking this thread, Joe will be checking this thread. We're understandably very busy so don't give up if we disappear for a day or two. Talk amongst yourselves while we're out of the room, as it were. But we will check in and try to answer questions. We want to hear from you. We want to know what you think.

So, go to it. And thanks for supporting Howard Dean.

About an hour later, after thirty responses appeared, Zephyr Teachout, Gross's colleague, chimed in with some answers. A little later, a participant on the site wrote: "This is too cool, an actual direct line to the Dean campaign committee! Pinch me—I must be dreaming!" Ultimately, more than four hundred people posted comments on Gross's thread. Richard Hoefer, a frequent visitor, later wrote me: "That was an amazing day to see that rise out of nowhere. People were floored that the thread title was 'Ask the Dean Campaign'—and Trippi and Matt were actually asking questions and interacting. Never before had anyone seen that."[1]

Jeff Tiedrich, the proprietor of the Smirking Chimp site (which he named satirically for President George W. Bush), told me, "It was amazing, for the first couple of weeks, that you could talk to a campaign inundated with thirty messages and queries a day. Frankly I thought they were nuts. I thought Rush Limbaugh would attack them for dissing the president. I was impressed by their foolhardiness."[2] So were hordes of Dean supporters, who saw a critical shift in the conventional workings of power in the candidate's willingness to engage directly and open up his campaign. By the summer of 2003, "people-powered Howard" had gathered a roiling grassroots network of supporters around his candidacy and shocked the political establishment by raising more money online than any of the leading candidates.

Today, the wall between powerful elected officials and the people they want to represent has started to come down. Political campaigns at every level make strenuous efforts to engage in direct and open dialogue with their supporters. They hold special conference calls for political bloggers, they do live chats on Facebook, they respond to direct questions on

Twitter, and they engage in video question-and-answer forums on YouTube. Much of this interactivity is aimed at showing that the candidate is "listening to the public" in the same way that a photo-op supposedly shows that a candidate cares about some issue, but sometimes they even give supporters tools to organize themselves on behalf of the campaign and invite them to help shape their agenda. This behavior has become so commonplace in politics that we've forgotten how big a cultural shift it represents.

The change isn't only coming from campaigns and other organizations or figures opening themselves up from the top down. It's also being created from the bottom up, as we literally carry in our pockets and on our laps the ability to connect and collaborate directly with each other, without requiring permission from the people formerly known as the authorities. And when you combine connectivity with transparency—the ability for more people to see, share, and shape what is going on around them—the result is a huge increase in social energy, which is being channeled in all kinds of directions.

I remember exactly when this light bulb went on for me. In 2002 and 2003, my younger brother David had started inviting me to come to trade shows for the open source software Linux; he had started a service company called LinuxCare, which aimed to provide reliable twenty-four-hour support to businesses using the upstart software platform. I didn't understand the technical conversations swirling around me at these events, but something about the crowd caught my attention. Was it the surprising number of ponytails on the mostly male programmers, most of whom were T-shirt-wearing baby boomers who looked like they would never be caught dead in a suit? Listening to programmer Eric Raymond give a talk on his book *The Cathedral and the Bazaar*, an early treatise on the value of open methods of collaborative development, I started to feel like I had stumbled upon a lost tribe from the 1960s.

The Linux development community, and the larger open source software movement that it was a part of, were in fact a branch of the 1960s counterculture that had run with the idea of personal empowerment into monumental success.[3] At the time, Linux was coming into its own as a reliable operating system that was free, unlike the dominant platform, Microsoft Windows. In addition, Linux was less likely to crash, less prone to viruses, and more efficient in its use of system resources. It was also rapidly eating into the market share of what was then the richest corporation in the world. The people who were making these tools were sharing ideas with each other in a manner I had never encountered in the political arena, even among members of the so-called "progressive community." And unlike my comrades from the political world, open source developers were embracing change. Their systems went through a literal reboot every few years. I was intrigued.

In early 2004, on assignment for *The Nation* to write about what I was starting to call "open source politics," I was in San Diego for the Digital Democracy Teach-In. The teach-in was a one-day event that was tacked onto the annual ETech confab, put on by Internet publisher Tim O'Reilly, who was soon to coin the term "Web 2.0." There on stage, was Dean's campaign manager Joe Trippi being interviewed by Ed Cone, an industry journalist who had done some in-depth pieces on the campaign. But alongside them, there was an LED screen labeled the "Hecklebot" projecting a constant stream of messages, some related to the conversation on stage, some not. I looked around. Of the four hundred or so people in the audience, at least half had their laptops open, and they weren't just taking notes. They were typing messages to each other, participating in a live chat-room using the conference's free Wi-Fi service. And their "back-channel" conversation—full of pithy and funny riffs on Trippi and Cone's talk, along with side jokes and questions about where to go out for lunch—was what was running on-stage, alongside the "official" conversation.

It was a disconcerting and exhilarating moment, showing me exactly how the Internet can give more people a voice in the public conversation and how lateral networking between tech-empowered individuals could open up a top-down forum (like a conference keynote) and make it into something far more interesting and participatory. Following along with both the main conversation and the back-channel, I quickly discovered that there were a lot of people in the room who had at least as much wisdom to offer as the speakers on stage. By seeing everyone's comments and joining in the give-and-take, I could even play a role in the public conversation we were all having. It didn't matter who I was or whether I had been credentialed by the "authorities" running the event as an expert. All that mattered was whether what I had to say had any credibility. I was now a full-fledged member of the group that NYU scholar Jay Rosen has dubbed "the people formerly known as the audience."[4]

Being connected in real-time also meant that we, the ex-audience, had a new ability to talk back to the powers that be, or as digital visionary Howard Rheingold likes to say, to be "crap-detectors" and "call bullshit" when we see it.[5] Nothing illustrates that better than a moment at the first Personal Democracy Forum in May 2004. Having caught the real-time interactivity bug from ETech, Andrew and I installed a similar online back channel at PdF. With the help of our friends David Isenberg and Greg Elin, we got the auditorium at the New School for Social Research wired for WiFi and set up a simple chat tool with a big screen on stage behind our panelists. But what happened next was magic.

During a panel on "Money, Votes, and Community,"

Republican lobbyist David Metzner said something to the effect of the Internet having democratized campaign fundraising and shifted politics away from fat cats to the little people. I was sitting next to my longtime colleague and friend Ellen Miller, who had started two groups focused on exposing and changing the role of big money in politics, the Center for Responsive Politics (CRP) and Public Campaign (which I had worked for from 1997 to 2003). We elbowed each other, and whispered that Metzner's claim was plainly contradicted by the facts. So, using my laptop, I wrote a comment into the public back-channel pointing out that most of the individual contributions to political campaigns come from just one-quarter of one percent of the population, and these people are almost entirely the wealthiest fraction of the population. All the 2004 campaigns, with the exception of Howard Dean's, were typically supported by people writing $2,000 checks, the maximum allowed. So much for the little people.

The audience started to murmur. I then turned to Ellen and said, Let's see if Metzner is himself a big donor. Again using my laptop, I went to OpenSecrets.org, CRP's website for tracking campaign donations. Seconds later, I was typing on the backchannel: Metzner himself is a fat cat, having given something like $78,000 to candidates and party committees over the last two election cycles. The audience started to laugh, pointing at the screen behind the panel. To his credit, Metzner stopped talking, looked behind him and said, "I have no problem with transparency. I'm proud of my campaign contributions." But now the audience heard everything he had to say about the Internet's impact on big money in politics in a very different light. It was a seminal moment, at least for Ellen and me.

By this point in 2004, lots of other people were also experiencing their own seminal moments. The 600,000 people who had put their hearts, minds, mousepads, and checkbooks together for Howard Dean and, at least for a time, driven a fairly obscure small-state governor to the center of the presidential campaign had just gotten a taste of their own power. "We all felt the muscle flex of this new progressive movement and were stunned by it," recalled Nicco Mele, Dean's webmaster.[6] Bloggers, the leaders of a new citizen journalism, were seeing their traffic multiply into the hundreds of thousands as readers flocked to sites that were more participatory and transparent than traditional media. People were learning how to ferret out information and force it into public view—and embarrassing all kinds of powerful targets, from Senator Trent Lott and CBS anchor Dan Rather to the Diebold electronic voting machine company, which tried to suppress the leak of embarrassing internal emails and instead saw them spread by activists onto hundreds of servers across the web.[7] (Shades of WikiLeaks!) And a new class of online organizers was taking shape—from MoveOn-style groups on the left to savvy e-campaign managers for President Bush's re-election—all discovering the power they could tap when they genuinely listened to their grassroots base and gave them meaningful ways to participate in the causes they cared about.

Transparency was the fuel; connectivity was the engine; a sense of oneself as a more effective participant in the democratic process (personal democracy, if you will) was the journey. What was emerging was a greatly expanded notion of the role of citizen not just as a passive consumer of political information and occasional voter, but as an active player, monitoring what government and politicians were doing, demanding a seat at the table and a view of the proceedings, sharing self-generated news of what was important, and participating in problem solving.

The back-channel was coming to the foreground. The modern transparency movement was about to take off.

3

From Scarcity to Abundance

You never change things by fighting the existing reality. To change something, build a new model that makes the existing model obsolete.

—R. Buckminster Fuller

The fundamental change powering the networked age of politics is the shift from scarcity to abundance. Thanks to the rapid evolution of computer processing power, all kinds of goods that were once expensive to produce have become cheap. Beyond the declining price of a personal computer or a backup drive, elemental changes in the economics of information, connectivity, and time have occurred:

- Information: The cost of making an electronic copy of any kind of data and sharing it with others has dropped to almost zero. This fact is remaking whole spheres of life, from the entertainment, news, and media businesses to all forms of social organization. Social sharing of data—be it MP3 files or once-secret government documents—is out of anyone's control once the material is in digital form. And anyone who wants to form an association of like-minded souls can do so in seconds, using search tools, social networks, or just plain old email.

- Connectivity: While there is still a limit to how many genuine connections one individual can have with others, there is no inherent limit to the number of connections that a community may create laterally. A "one-to-many" email list or social following may look valuable (think of Barack Obama's thirteen-million-strong 2008 campaign email address list), but no one person can have millions of personal relationships. A "many-to-many" network, however, can have millions, even billions, of intimate ties. Thus, while leaders and celebrities remain important, their stars are dimming, as community hubs, forums, and aggregators that knit together thousands or even hundreds of thousands of people are steadily growing.

- Time: As the price of memory and disk space has continued to collapse, our ability to share time-intensive and content-rich resources has exploded. Thus while old media like television, radio, and print have inherent physical limits on how much space or time than can give to any subject, on the Internet there are no such limits. The sound bite can be replaced with a sound blast, and if your content is compelling, people will share it for you.

The explosion of capacity means that old practices of hoarding or hiding information, done sometimes for pragmatic reasons (it was too costly to make lots of copies) and other times to maintain a position of privilege, now seem like artificial barriers to access. Across our culture, people and institutions that open themselves even partially to this new expectation of participation and transparency are beating out those who hold to the old ways. Television is now riddled with reality shows that invite regular audience participation. News sites are requiring their reporters to accept comments on their articles, seeing how bloggers have been drawing away their readers with their more interactive platforms. Publishers who build hubs for aggregating all kinds of raw data and invite their readers to help bubble up the best stuff are earning huge traffic, beating out the older model of tight editorial gatekeeping in advance of publication.[1] All kinds of businesses, from airlines and computer retailers to supermarket chains and cable conglomerates, are interacting with their customers using tools like Twitter.[2]

In this new context, a political campaign that refuses to engage supporters in an interactive manner is now seen as overly controlling. A legislature that makes public documents available solely by printing them in binders and making people come to a basement office in the Capitol, rather than posting them online in searchable, downloadable form, is seen as being ridiculously secretive.[3] Charging exorbitant fees to access public information, or preventing people from contributing their own knowledge, is seen as hopelessly behind the times. And a government body that monopolizes control of public data not only risks undermining public trust in its actions. It also stands to lose out in the burgeoning new world of participatory democracy known as "we-government," where citizens are using connective technologies and public data to create whole new ways of identifying and solving civic problems.

There has always been an informal sector of society where people shared information and resources with each other on a voluntary and self-organized basis. Think of church suppers, rent parties, barn-raisings, and clubs for all types of amateurs passionate about something. What the new economics of abundant information, connectivity, and time make possible are barn-raising projects at much larger scale. Consider the following chart:

| | Value-System | |
	$	♡
Centralized	Firms	Government Non-profits
Decentralized	"The Market"	Informal Community

(left axis: Mode of Organization)

Across the top are two kinds of value systems that we use to order our decisions. Sometimes, we let money and such concerns as "return on investment" or supply and demand determine the value of an activity, or a person. Other times, we make decisions on nonmarket values such as love, charity, or solidarity. Different kinds of institutions serve those different values; they may be centralized, like firms and government entities or nonprofit organizations, or they may be decentralized, like the anarchic marketplace or the face-to-face worlds of our local communities and ad hoc self-organizing.

This last sector, the fourth one, has until recently been too small to matter. Church suppers and rent parties and social clubs have always existed, but only at local scale. Now, thanks to the Internet, we are seeing fourth sector entities at national, even global scale. (I am indebted to Yochai Benkler and his book, *The Wealth of Networks*, for this analysis.)

For example, Wikipedia started in 2001. The nonprofit site, which describes itself as a "free encyclopedia that anyone can edit," is written collaboratively by online volunteers. The English version has more than 3.5 million articles that have been edited more than 435 million times by more than thirteen million registered users. A much smaller core group of less than 2,000 volunteer administrators act as trusted editors of the site, who watch over pages and guard the site from digital vandals. The Wikimedia Foundation, which keeps Wikipedia's servers running—no small task now that the site is one of the top destinations for traffic worldwide—has a paid staff of about fifty people. But the bulk of the work on Wikipedia is done by people who donate their time and expertise. The site takes no advertising and relies completely on donations.

Or take the DailyKos.com political blog, started by Iraq War army veteran Markos Moulitsas in 2002, which now has a paid staff of eight. Currently the site has more than 250,000 registered users, each of whom has the power to post their own diaries or comment on others on the site. About two thousand individual diaries are written on it each day, with less than one percent of the content contributed by Moulitsas himself. It gets about a half million daily visitors. Even though it has a huge number of users and arguably has grown way past any kind of community level of intimacy, it continues to grow at the rate of about two hundred new registrants a day, and many of them become active contributors to the site's daily content.

It would be a mistake to think of DailyKos as just another political blog, however. The site is more like a midsize, virtual city. Its primary focus is politics to be sure—participants are expected to stick to Moulitsas's founding vision of a hub for progressive Democrats who want to rebuild their party, elect more Democrats to office, and win more progressive policy victories wherever possible. But while the DailyKos front page functions like a huge collaboration engine or switchboard, where every participant's diary gets a few seconds of visibility and the best ones get voted on to the recommended list, where they can garner thousands of comments and tens of thousands of views, the site is also a thriving and intimate network of many little villages. A close observer will find:

- A Sunday night prayer/meditation section called "Brothers and Sisters";
- A Monday evening page called "The Grieving Room" for members who have lost or are about to lose a loved one;
- A Wednesday morning recipe-sharing club called "Iron Chef Kos";
- A Wednesday evening book club;
- A Friday afternoon forum called "Frugal Fridays," where members share moneysaving tips and talk about personal finance issues;
- A Saturday morning gardening club;
- A Saturday morning home repair group;
- A Saturday morning parenting diary;
- A "Saturday Night Loser's Club" for people who couldn't get a date that night; and
- A Sunday morning puzzle sharing group.

How else has DailyKos managed to keep its intimate feeling while growing to the size of a large American city? One answer comes from the dozens of daily volunteers who read diaries posted by newcomers and perform "diary rescue"—that is, they write summaries of the best posts submitted each day and give those rescued diaries some front-page attention. That way a newcomer to the site is likely to be rewarded for contributing their thoughts by receiving some attention from the whole community, which usually come in the form of complimentary comments. The result? When I attended the first face-to-face meeting of the Kos community, at a convention center in Las Vegas in June 2006 where more than two thousand people attended, the main hall felt like a summer camp reunion of people who knew each other personally (either by name or user handle) but had never met before.

This style of political organizing is not the monopoly of the left; the Internet itself is just a system that rewards open methods more than closed ones. The Tea Party movement in United States, at least in some of its iterations, is another good example of open source organizing. Instead of having one central address or leader, it has lots of small groups and no real barrier to entry. Thus no one can control it or stop it by delegitimizing a single leader.[4] "If you have a machine, you know exactly how to attack it, exactly how to shut it down," says Keli Carender, an early Tea Party activist from Seattle. "If you have three million machines coming at you, you don't know where to turn."[5] As Jonathan Rauch wrote in a long article describing the movement's methods:

> The tea party began as a network, not an organization, and that
> is what it mostly remains. Disillusioned with President Bush's
> Republicans and disheartened by President Obama's election, in

late 2008 several dozen conservatives began chattering on social-networking sites such as Top Conservatives on Twitter and Smart Girl Politics. Using those resources and frequent conference calls (the movement probably could not have arisen before the advent of free conference calling), they began to talk about doing something. What they didn't realize was that they were already doing something. In the very act of networking, they were printing the circuitry for a national jolt of electricity.

The spark came on February 19, 2009, when a CNBC journalist named Rick Santelli aired a diatribe against the bank bailout. "That," [Tea Party Patriots national co-coordinator Mark] Meckler says, "was our source code." The next day, the networkers held a conference call and decided to stage protests in a few cities just a week later. No one was more astonished than the organizers when the network produced rallies in about fifty cities, organized virtually overnight by amateurs. Realizing that they had opened a vein, they launched a second round of rallies that April, this time turning out perhaps 600,000 people at more than 600 events. . . .

By the summer of 2009, tea parties were springing up all over. Multitudes of activists, operatives, and groups were claiming the tea party mantle, many of them at odds with or suspicious of each other. Believing that coordination was needed, an ad hoc committee emerged from among the core group and, by August of last year, had opened a bank account under the spontaneously chosen name of the Tea Party Patriots.[6]

The Tea Party Patriots is now incorporated as a nonprofit political organization with a staff of less than ten people. Its website claims several thousand local affiliates and a total membership of 15 million people. Even if those numbers are exaggerated (and I believe that they are, probably by a factor of ten),[7] and even if the movement benefits from behind-the-scenes support from wealthy backers and the lavish attention of the Fox News Network, this is still a huge mobilization of grassroots energy.

What loose, networked communities like Wikipedia, DailyKos, and the Tea Party are all drawing on is a growing pool of networked citizens who want to do more than just consume information, they want to help create it and shape it, too. In the United States, for example, the Pew Internet & American Life Project estimates that roughly seventy-nine percent of all American adults are Internet users, meaning they go online or use email at least occasionally. Among Americans aged eighteen to forty-nine, the proportion tops ninety percent.[8] While there is still a digital divide in America, it is primarily older people who are least likely to go online, and poorer and more rural Americans who lack affordable access to high-speed broadband. The digital disconnect is unlikely to dramatically improve for the elderly, but as more mobile phones come equipped with fast connections to the web, the gap will disappear for nearly everyone else.

In October 2008, one-third of Americans said their main source for political information was the Internet—more than triple the number from four years ago, according to Pew. Among younger Americans, people aged between eighteen and twenty-nine, forty-nine percent said the Internet was their main source of political news.[9] Voter-generated content now rivals professional media for the public's attention. As of the fall of 2008, nearly one in four said they had watched a homemade video about the election.[10] One study estimated that more than 160,000 videos mentioning Barack Obama or John McCain were uploaded to the web, with nearly 1.5 billion views. Videos made directly by the two presidential campaigns only garnered ten percent of that total number of views.[11]

We're in the midst of a revolution in media participation, not just news consumption. To be sure, the vast majority of Americans do not choose to actively participate in politics on a daily basis. People are more likely to check the news than they are to make the news. But while most Americans still treat politics as a spectator sport, according to the Pew Center on the Internet & American Life's research, somewhere between fifteen and twenty-five million of us are what Pew calls "online political activists" or the "government participatory class."[12] That is, people actively engaged each day in sifting the news, sharing our concerns and steering each other—and the rest of the citizenry—towards actions aimed at shifting the debate.

In 2008, the energies of this group tilted to the advantage of Barack Obama. Obama voters were far more likely than McCain voters to engage in online politicking; Pew's survey data found that they were nearly three times as likely to sign up online to volunteer for the campaign; two and a half times as likely to donate money; twice as likely to sign up for email election alerts; and significantly more likely to share online videos or text messages with other voters. One-quarter of online Obama voters posted their opinions on a blog, email list, or social networking site, compared to just fifteen percent of McCain supporters.[13]

In 2010, the tables turned. The "right-roots" were fast to adopt the newer online platforms, especially after the GOP lost its hold on Congress and the White House. Pew's 2010 survey found that Republican and Democratic voters were equally likely to use social networking sites. In some cases, such as their use of the Internet to post political content, get candidate information or "friend" a candidate or cause, Republicans were significantly more likely to do so than Democrats.[14] As last fall's elections approached, Republican Senate candidates had tallied more than 1.4 million fans on Facebook, compared to only 300,000 for Democrats; and 520,000 followers on Twitter, compared to just 90,000 for the Democrats, a clear sign of the enthusiasm gap between the parties.[15]

The data for the rest of the world is less detailed, but the trend lines are similar. Between one-third and two-fifths of the adults in Poland, Britain, South Korea, France, Spain, Russia, and Brazil use social networking sites, according to a twenty-two-nation survey by the Pew Global Attitudes Project—which is only a tad below Americans' level of usage (forty-six percent). In twelve countries, a majority under the age of thirty uses those sites. Mobile phone ownership is also up, to a median rate of eighty-one percent across sixteen countries with current data.[16] Though political participation varies enormously from country to country, depending on a host of local conditions, rules, and history, the overall shift is the same.

In places like Tunisia, Egypt, Jordan, and Yemen, which have been rocked in recent months by youth-driven political uprisings, the degree of Internet penetration, social network usage, and mobile phone ownership may not matter as much as more basic factors like demographics, unemployment rates, and education levels. Satellite TV networks like Al-Jazeera, which offer a radically different point of view from state-run media, are also vital to spurring social change movements in this countries. But there's plenty of evidence pointing to the value of social networking tools in the democracy movements underway.

In Egypt, for example, a limited degree of press and internet freedom allowed young activists to build online support around human rights cases, most notably with a Facebook group focused on striking workers called the "April 6 Youth Movement," which gained 70,000 supporters in 2008, and another group called "We Are All Khaled Said" dedicated to a twenty-eight-year-old businessman beaten to death by police, which quickly drew 130,000 online supporters in 2009. A video said to be made by Said showing corrupt police officers was viewed more than half a million times on YouTube, another vital channel for these growing movements.

After the protests in Tunisia exploded, the Egyptian activists running these two Facebook groups called on their supporters to come into the streets on January 25; the rest is history.[17]

Abundant information, connectivity, and time are just the technical ingredients needed to foster an explosion of civic activity; it is the growing presence of this huge and dynamic mass of people that is actually driving the changes we are living through. It helps, of course, that the Internet is a "lean forward" medium full of invitations to join, participate, and create your own content, compared to the "lean back" media of television, radio, and newsprint. As Tom Matzzie, onetime director of online organizing for the AFL-CIO and then for MoveOn, once said to me, "You can't buy your way to success on the Internet. You can't buy a twenty percent open rate on your emails. You have to be the real deal."[18]

But we now live in an age of abundant public energies, in addition to abundant information, connectivity and time. Instead of wasting all of our leisure time on private pleasures or passive consumption, more and more of us are being drawn into constructive civic projects, many of them reaching impressive scale. To return to Wikipedia, you wouldn't be alone if you wondered how all those millions of people could possibly have the time to add their edits and help tend to the site. The social theorist Clay Shirky offers a compelling answer with his idea of the "cognitive surplus":

So if you take Wikipedia as a kind of unit, all of Wikipedia, the whole project—every page, every edit, every talk page, every line of code, in every language that Wikipedia exists in—that represents something like the accumulation of one hundred million hours of human thought. I worked this out with Martin Wattenberg at IBM; it's a back-of-the-envelope calculation, but it's the right order of magnitude, about one hundred million hours of thought.

And television watching? Two hundred billion hours, in the U.S. alone, every year. Put another way, now that we have a unit, that's 2,000 Wikipedia projects a year spent watching television. Or put still another way, in the U.S., we spend one hundred million hours every weekend, just watching the ads. This is a pretty big surplus. People asking, "Where do they find the time?" when they're looking at things like Wikipedia don't understand how tiny that entire project is. . . .

And this is the other thing about the size of the cognitive surplus we're talking about. It's so large that even a small change could have huge ramifications. Let's say that everything stays ninety-nine percent the same, that people watch ninety-nine percent as much television as they used to, but one percent of that is carved out for producing and for sharing. The Internet-connected population watches roughly a *trillion* hours of TV a year. That's about five times the size of the annual U.S. consumption. One percent of that is one hundred Wikipedia projects per year worth of participation.[19]

John Perry Barlow's infowar has begun in earnest, because a significant portion of the population that is leaning forward and choosing to produce and share information—a piece of this gigantic cognitive surplus, if you will—has decided that we would like to know what is actually going on.

4

Kicking Down the Door to the Smoke-Filled Room

Transparency is the new objectivity.

—David Weinberger, author of
Small Pieces, Loosely Joined,
speaking at Personal Democracy Forum June 2009[1]

If the transparency movement in the United States has
a modern father, his name is Carl Malamud. In the early
1990s, Malamud was running a nonprofit called the Internet
Multicasting Service. A small controversy arose between
public-interest advocates and the Securities and Exchange
Commission over access to the commission's EDGAR
(Electronic Data Gathering, Analysis, and Retrieval) database
of filings from public corporations and other financial
institutions. At that time, the only way to access these files
was either by going to a special reading room in Washington,
or subscribing to an expensive private information service
like Mead Data's Nexis service, which charged $15 per

document, plus a connection charge of $39 per hour. So Malamud got a $660,000 two-year grant from the National Science Foundation to "develop and demonstrate ways to post large government data archives on the Internet for access by researchers and the general public." (The SEC staff and its contractor claimed that it would cost $18 million to provide such a service.) Included in the proposal was the promise to develop public domain software enabling a way for users to search the data over the Internet. At the time, just twenty million people had Internet access in the United States.[2]

After wading through some congressional resistance kicked up by Rep. John Dingell, an ally of the private information providers, Malamud's service launched on January 17, 1994. At first, the data he made available was two days old, a result of the time it took for the SEC to overnight the data disks to his office and then for them to be uploaded. But users streamed to it nonetheless, as many as 50,000 a day. As Malamud recounted at a keynote address at the 2009 Government 2.0 Summit in Washington, "What we found when we placed these so-called products on the Internet—for free—was that these reports were not just fodder for a few well-heeled financial professionals, a commodity used to make the Wall Street money machine function, but instead that these public reports of public corporations were of tremendous interest to journalists, students, senior citizen investment clubs, employees of the companies reporting and employees of their competitors, in short a raft of new uses that had been impossible before."[3]

By late 1994, other partners were joining in Malamud's quirky venture. MIT, NYU, Sun Microsystems, MCI Communications, R. R. Donnelly & Sons, and Time Inc. announced they were working to expand the databases provided to include patents, trademarks, and all current SEC filings. As Vint Cerf, one of the creators of the Internet (who was then at MCI and now works for Google as its senior Internet evangelist), said at the time, "I think the rest of the world is listening to how valuable it is for a government to provide information to its citizens."[4] By the summer of 1995, Malamud was providing SEC records on a same-day basis, thanks to donations from two private companies. But in the fall, his NSF grant was due to run out and Malamud prepared to pull the plug.

What he did next was ingenious. In mid-August, two months before his funding was to expire, Malamud posted a headline banner on the Internet Multicasting Service site, announcing that he would stop the free EDGAR service at the beginning of October. But he offered to give his software to the SEC and train its staff to continue the service directly. In an inspired touch, he posted contact information so that users could click to send an email to the commission's chairman, Arthur Levitt, as well as public officials like then House Speaker Newt Gingrich and Vice President Al Gore, both of whom were themselves advocating making more government information available online. Soon the agency capitulated, took over from Malamud, and started making this vital trove of information available to the public for free.

Malamud was a pioneer in liberating taxpayer-financed public information and putting it online where everyone could get to it. He has continued to fight for expanding free access to public domain material online, convincing C-SPAN to open up its congressional video archives, digitizing old government films for the Internet Archive, and making troves of court decisions and legal documents available. And his work has been at the forefront of a wave of new efforts—from the Library of Congress's Thomas database of congressional bills and votes, and the Center for Responsive Politics OpenSecrets.org database of campaign finance information, to the Environmental Working Group's searchable database of individual agricultural subsidy recipients—that all sought to make public records more accessible. Each of these efforts has succeeded in demonstrating the public hunger for more information about government's activities, as well as the ins and outs of who was influencing and benefiting from its decisions.

But for about the first ten years of the World Wide Web, from roughly 1995 to 2005, public records were usually locked in formats that limited how people could make use of them. Sometimes all that was available was summary data, rather than the individual records. Other times, records were placed online as scanned PDF files, which made them impossible to search and difficult to link to. You could look up a contributor name in the Federal Election Commission database, but you'd get dozens of unsearchable PDF files in return. A link to a bill on Thomas would expire once you closed your search, making it impossible for bloggers to link to the actual text of bills. And good luck trying to find in one place a member's actual voting record, or a digitized version of their annual personal financial disclosure report. It was a far cry from the promise Newt Gingrich made as he was becoming speaker of the House in 1994 to make changes so that congressional information "will be available to any citizen in the country at the same moment that it is available to the highest paid Washington lobbyist."[5]

These approaches started to change only in the last few years, as technologists and public-interest advocates alike began to understand the power of open standards for sharing data. A breakthrough moment came in early 2005. At that time a 3-D graphic artist named Paul Rademacher built a free online application called HousingMaps by combining real estate listings from Craigslist with city street maps from Google Maps. He built it to make his own housing hunt easier, by showing him on a map where apartments he could afford were located. His hack, or "mash-up," wasn't exactly authorized by either Craigslist or Google, but neither company put tight restrictions on the use of their data, and Google was soon to open up a public application programming interface (or API), that was designed to allow people to build sites and services on top of their mapping tool.

Still, no one had quite imagined what would happen once independent developers started playing with the new capabilities of the web. Google employees wrote on a company web page that HousingMaps "blew our minds right off our shoulders."[6] Longtime technology guru Tim O'Reilly called Rademacher's site "the first true Web 2.0 application," and indeed once people saw the possibilities, a wave of innovation exploded around the possibilities of dynamically combining data and visualizations in amazing new ways. One might say that at the same time political organizing on the web was getting more social, as discussed in the previous chapter, the uses of data online were also getting more interactive.

Writing later that year, O'Reilly condensed the core ideas of "Web 2.0" in an essay that had a lot of influence on the transparency movement.[7] The three concepts that stood out were a) thinking of the web as a platform, b) looking for ways to harness collective intelligence and c) making data services the centerpiece:

- The web as a platform: instead of building websites as destinations for information-seekers, successful Web 2.0 innovators provide information in forms that can be taken anywhere on the web. Thus, a tool like Google

Maps can be implemented anywhere, not just on a "GoogleMaps.com" site.

- Harnessing collective intelligence: Web 2.0 services are designed to tap the wisdom of the crowd. Google's search engine ranks pages based on how many other pages link to them, and it learns from what links people click which pages offer the best results to a particular search phrase. Wikipedia harnesses the power-of-many by allowing anyone to add or edit any page. Picture-sharing sites like Flickr let anyone make up their own tags for content, rather than forcing people to only use categories chosen from above. In each case, network effects make these services more valuable as they gain more users.

- Data is "the next Intel inside": successful Web 2.0 companies win in their fields not only by cornering some class of data (location, product identifiers, namespaces) but by also making their data the underpinning of a whole range of additional services. For example, Amazon didn't just build its books database on top of a proprietary tracking tool known as the ISBN number; it added new data (cover images, table of contents) and, crucially, invited its users to add their own (reviews, ratings). Eventually, Amazon created its own identifier, the ASIN, which it extended to all kinds of products, and built an API to let others build services on top of that.

Inspired by these ideas and trends, in the fall and winter of 2005-06 I worked together with my PdF colleague Andrew Rasiej in advising our friends Ellen Miller and Michael Klein as they set up the Sunlight Foundation, the first Washington-based nonprofit dedicated to using technology and the Internet to open up government. Ellen, as noted earlier, had a long background in political reform work. Mike came from the world of business, where for many years he was a successful securities lawyer. But he was fed up with the amount of influence peddling and corruption that permeated Washington, and wanted to "give back" something of his personal fortune to help make Congress more accountable to the people. With the words of Supreme Court Justice Louis Brandeis ringing in our ears—"Sunlight is said to be the best of disinfectants; electric light the most efficient policeman"— and a generous initial donation from Mike, Sunlight officially opened its doors on April 24, 2006.

"Sunlight's goal," wrote Ellen, "is to provide tools, information and resources to encourage citizens, bloggers and investigative media to explore whether and/or how their representatives are influenced by money and lobbyists, to provide ways to engage their natural curiosity about who their representatives really represent and what they do in Washington, and to provide forums and interactions to build the community of people who care about our democracy."[8] Early on, Sunlight supported the development of sites like

Congresspedia, a wiki anyone could edit focused on members of Congress and their work; MapLight, a research tool for exploring the possible correlations between campaign contributions and legislative votes; and OpenCongress, a unified hub that enables users to track members, bills, votes, and issues, and to see what items were being most viewed, or most talked about in the news and on blogs. Sunlight also funded the digitization of records like congressional financial disclosure statements, foreign lobbyist registrations, and earmarks; helped longtime money-in-politics repositories OpenSecrets.org (federal data) and FollowtheMoney.org (state-by-state data) open source all their individual records; and built new resources, like a real-time database of congressional fundraisers and a ticker alerting users to new lobbyist registrations.

The Sunlight Foundation wasn't the only group moving in this direction. A small but steadily growing community of politically minded hackers and technologically savvy activists were also hard at work, some on their own for years and others who soon joined this burgeoning movement. In 2004, a linguistics graduate student named Joshua Tauberer single-handedly took on the task of making it easy to access and work with the latest information from the U.S. Congress. His site, GovTrack.us, was just a hobby when he started it, but over time it grew into a critical resource. Since Congress actually wasn't making its information available to the public in anything like a computationally useful form, Tauberer built data scrapers that pull information automatically off of Thomas and then convert it into forms other computer programmers can use.

In England, a scrappy band of coders that called themselves mySociety.org were ahead of everyone else. Led by a former civil servant named Tom Steinberg, mySociety focused on building deceptively simple websites aimed at helping people improve their civic lives, while also teaching the public sector how it could use the Internet more efficiently to make a difference in people's lives. While mySociety doesn't sound like a transparency operation, the power of opening and sharing data is central to its work. Before mySociety was officially started in the fall of 2003, several of its founders had previously built a little site called FaxMyMP, which enabled anyone to type in their postcode, get the name of their member of Parliament, and then type in a message, which got delivered to them as a fax. But, ingeniously, the site also asked users to report back how long it took their elected representatives to respond, and published comprehensive tables charting their relative performance.[9] This bit of user-generated transparency has had the beneficial effect of getting many members to be more responsive to their constituents.

Another overlapping group of mySociety volunteers built an even more impressive site called TheyWorkForYou, which launched in 2004. The site combines records from all of Great

Britain's parliamentary bodies, and enables anyone to track a member's interests, voting record, election results—even how often they speak on the floor. Its tracking methods were so accurate, and the visibility of the rankings so high, members started changing their speaking behavior in an effort to game the system and improve their rating.[10] All of mySociety's web projects are imbued with this same wisdom: while providing a basic service that helps people in their lives, the users and the website create meta-data that also can leverage changes in how the institutions of government and society behave. FixMyStreet collects and sends reports of local problems to local officials, but also shows users which city councils are, or aren't, being responsive to fixing them. WhatDoTheyKnow helps users file Freedom of Information requests to the government, but then collects and makes searchable all the answers that flow back.

Eric Raymond, one of the earliest evangelists for the open source software movement, famously wrote that the ethos of the first developer of Linux, Linus Torvalds, was "given enough eyeballs, all bugs are shallow."[11] In technical terms, this means that if you have enough early testers of your software, and you make the source code visible, the community as a whole can easily help spot problems and help solve them. The same notion has come to apply, again and again, to the transparency movement. If you make a problem visible, or put it out on the web in a form that lots of people can swarm around, often a solution will be found. "Crowdsourcing" is the term often used to describe this process, though I think it's somewhat of a misnomer. We aren't outsourcing a job that used to belong to professionals (such as investigative journalists) and giving it to a crowd to do; we're inviting lots of civic watchdogs to add their eyeballs and time to the process of making government more transparent and accountable. Call it crowd-scouring instead.

From its early days, the transparency movement has had lots of crowd-scouring successes. For example, a mostly libertarian- and conservative-led group of bloggers calling themselves the Porkbusters got going in the wake of Hurricane Katrina in 2005 by asking their readers to help identify wasteful government projects that could be cut to find extra money to help with the disaster recovery effort. Their biggest victory came the next year, when they teamed up with liberal blogger Joshua Marshall to back a proposed bipartisan bill to create the first-ever official federal database of all government contracts and grants. The Federal Accountability and Transparency Act of 2006, cosponsored by then-Senator Barack Obama and Republican Senator Tom Coburn, had been stymied by a so-called "secret hold" placed on it by an unknown senator. With some help from the Sunlight Foundation, this cross-partisan coalition of bloggers asked their readers to call their individual senators to ask if they were the guilty party. Within days, the culprits—Senators Ted

Stevens and Robert Byrd—had been unmasked, and lifted their objections. The bill then passed unanimously and was signed into law.

In a first for a blogger, Marshall and his site Talking Points Memo (TPM) won a major journalism award for an even larger and harder crowd-scouring project, his investigation into the politically driven firings of United States Attorneys during the Bush administration. He and his writers noticed that two district attorneys from different parts of the country were being dismissed for seemingly odd reasons, and they asked their readers for help looking for similar stories in local media. Eventually they discovered a clear pattern, well ahead of the national press. They also asked readers again and again for help reading through huge document dumps put out by the administration.[12] As Marshall wrote on his blog, "Some of the most exciting projects we (and I mean, TPM and a large group of regular readers) have done over the years would never have been possible without the Internet's distributed communication tools and the various fee-based (Nexis) and public databases (google, fec.gov) we'd never have ready access to with the Net. Add all that social networking and information together and you get a big leap forward in what you can find out and what you can do about it."[13] Marshall and Co.'s distributed digging eventually led to the resignation of Attorney General Alberto Gonzales.

The grassroots government-transparency movement has

branched in many directions in recent years. In 2007, in a first for courtroom transparency, a rotating team of six bloggers from FireDogLake.com live-blogged the Scooter Libby trial, providing real-time coverage that the rest of the media didn't see as a priority, but came to rely on. (Libby, Vice President Dick Cheney's chief of staff, was convicted for obstructing justice and perjury in the Valerie Plame affair, which ironically enough was about the unauthorized leaking of classified information. President Bush commuted his prison sentence.) At the time, NYU press critic Jay Rosen marveled:

> That an online community could, of its own free will, scare up support for six correspondents at a big trial; that the correspondents would work as hard as they did informing a live public; that they did it for expenses (no pay) and the joy of informing people who depend on you, this is a small, but remarkable part of the Libby case to reflect on, if we're still aftermathing it. What makes it possible are the people who gather at the site, and the falling cost for those people to meet up, realize their number, find a common mind, and when necessary pool their dollars to get their own correspondents to Washington.[14]

Citizen reporters interested in helping broaden and deepen coverage of the 2008 presidential campaign also volunteered their time on the Huffington Post's "Off the Bus" Project (which Rosen helped launch and direct); some 2,000 of them produced reports that were posted on the site, and a handful, like Mayhill Fowler's report from inside an Obama fundraiser, where he described some rural Americans as "bitter" about losing their jobs and "cling[ing] to guns or religion," made national news.

In a different kind of crowd-scouring effort that started in the summer of 2009, volunteers swarmed over congressional earmark requests in a project led by libertarian Jim Harper's WashingtonWatch.com site (with some support from the Sunlight Foundation). As Harper wrote when he launched the effort:

> For years now, earmarking has been conducted behind the scenes, but the House and Senate recently required their membership to reveal earmark requests. The door to the smoke-filled room has been unlocked, and now we're going to kick it down! The problem is that earmark information is spread out across congressional Web sites, and it's in many different formats. The solution? We've created a system for compiling earmark data in one place—actually, for you to compile it. We want you to add earmarks to our database through our earmark entry form. Pick your hometown member of Congress or Senator, your favorite representative—or your least favorite—and put their earmarks in the database.[15]

In just five days, volunteers inputted more than 5,000 earmarks into WashingtonWatch's database.[16] Ultimately, EarmarkData.org catalogued more than 40,000 earmark requests for 2010. In 2010, working with help from Taxpayers for Common Sense and Taxpayers Against Earmarks, about 39,000 requests totaling $130 billion were tallied and posted online in a searchable database.

Similarly, when a complete raw database of more

than 450,000 expense records for members of the British Parliament was leaked to the media that same summer, *The Guardian* asked its readers for help sifting through them. More than 27,000 people pitched in, reading and annotating more than 220,000 of them. Together, this crowd of citizen-journalist volunteers produced an incredibly detailed spreadsheet itemizing the actual spending totals, breaking down the average amounts by party membership and type of expenditure (kitchen, garden, TV, carpet, etc).[17] The uproar—which owes much to the more traditional watchdogging efforts of freelance journalist Heather Brooke, who diligently kept making requests under Britain's nascent Freedom of Information law to obtain the records—ultimately led to the resignation of the speaker of the House of Commons and several members of both houses, criminal proceedings against some members and government officials, and dramatic promises of increased transparency from the leaders of Britain's major parties.

Finally, no look at grassroots activism around transparency issues would be complete without covering the fight over the Wall Street bailout. Popular interest in the details of this gigantic transfer of wealth was evident from the moment the U.S. House of Representatives posted the text of its proposed $700 billion bill the week of September 29, 2008. The deluge of people trying to access www.house.gov and send emails to their members of Congress crashed the site. "We haven't seen this much demand since the 9-11 commission report was posted on the site in 2004," said a spokesman for the House Chief Administrative Officer. Tuesday of that week, one day after the House voted down the first version of the bailout bill, House web administrators had to impose a limit on the number of incoming emails that could be processed by the "Write Your Representative" function of the site. "This measure has become temporarily necessary to ensure that Congressional websites are not completely disabled by the millions of emails flowing into the system," they told member offices.

Demand for the text of the legislation was so intense that third-party sites that track Congress were also swamped. GovTrack.us, Josh Tauberer's website, had to shut down. "So many people are searching for the economic relief bill that GovTrack can't handle it," Tauberer posted. "Take a break and come back later when the world cools off." OpenCongress.org also reported a record number of 120,000 page views in one day. And once people got their hands on the bill's text, they tore into it with zeal. Nearly a thousand comments were posted on PublicMarkup.org, a site set up by the Sunlight Foundation to enable the public to examine and debate the text of the proposed legislation. Thousands of bloggers zeroed in on the extraneous earmarks in the bill, like a reduction in taxes on wooden arrow manufacturers. Others focused on members who voted for the bill, analyzing their campaign contributors and arguing that Wall Street donations influenced their vote.[18]

Public interest didn't let up. When, during an oversight hearing, Rep. Alan Grayson peppered Elizabeth Coleman, the inspector general of the Federal Reserve, with questions about where all the trillions pumped into Wall Street firms actually went, the YouTube video of their exchange garnered more than three million views, perhaps the most for any congressional hearing ever. Matt Stoller, who was then Grayson's senior policy adviser, argues that the whole conversation about financial policy changed radically during this period, as rising public attention lifted a raft of new financial bloggers into view. "Whereas at the beginning of the financial panic in 2007–2008, the Fed was a sole provider of expertise and credibility on finance to the political class, by 2010, the new financial blogosphere destroyed the Fed's mythic stature," he writes. "It is common for staffers to get more and better information from blogs, and for hearings to be driven by the conversation online, than from the Congressional liaison group at the Fed."[19] Ultimately activists ranging from followers of libertarian Ron Paul on the right to supporters of Grayson and Senator Bernie Sanders on the left also succeeded in 2010 in forcing Congress to adopt a new law requiring the Federal Reserve to detail all the recipients of bailout funding during the banking crisis.

That last victory was substantial. The *Wall Street Journal* editorial page praised the results of the Federal Reserve's new transparency, writing:

> Lender of last resort indeed. The Federal Reserve pulled back the curtain yesterday on its emergency lending during the financial panic of 2008 and 2009, and the game to play at home with the kids is: who didn't get a bailout? If you can find a big financial player who declined the Fed's cash, you're doing better than we did yesterday afternoon.
>
> The documents aren't another WikiLeaks dump but are due to Vermont Senator Bernie Sanders, who insisted that the Dodd-Frank financial bill require more transparency about how the Fed allocated capital during the panic. The release of this data on some 21,000 Fed transactions over the last three years is one of the rare useful provisions in Dodd-Frank, but kudos to our favorite Socialist for demanding it.
>
> We learn, for example, that the cream of Wall Street received even more multibillion-dollar assistance than previously advertised by either the banks or the Fed. Goldman Sachs used the Primary Dealer Credit Facility eighty-five times to the tune of nearly $600 billion. Even in Washington, that's still a lot of money. Morgan Stanley used the same overnight lending program 212 times from March 2008 to March 2009. This news makes it impossible to argue that either bank would have survived the storm without the Fed's cash.[20]

It's been said that the Internet interprets censorship as failure and routes around it. In fact, it is people using the Internet who interpret secrecy as a democratic failure—as a reason not to trust government—and more and more we route around it until we get at the truth.

5

The Global Transparency Movement

Hum Janenge—Hum Jiyenge
(The right to know is the right to live)
                        —*Slogan of India's National Campaign for*
                        People's Right to Information movement[1]

Last May, I had dinner in Vienna with Marko Rakar, the
founder of the Croatian blog Pollitika.com. Less than a month
earlier, he had been arrested and briefly detained by the police
on suspicion of posting a secret list of 501,666 veterans from
the 1991–95 Balkan war. The disclosure of the list provoked
an immediate uproar in the country, as millions of people
went looking for the records of people they knew, as well
as prominent national figures. Outrage followed as readers
discovered that some public figures who had never served in
the military were receiving lucrative veterans' benefits like
premium health care and duty-free car imports, and that
about 20,000 people had been registered as veterans despite
serving fifteen days or less in the military. As there were only
326,000 vets on the list a year after the war ended, many

Croatians suspect that thousands have illegally obtained veterans' benefits through corruption and bribery. The site, RegistrarBranitelja.com, which is based in the United States, received more than twelve million visits in just a few weeks, an astounding number for a country of just 4.5 million people, and crashed several times from the load.

Rakar denies that he posted the leaked veterans registry database, and the police never found any evidence that he did. But if you say to him, "Well, nobody knows how it was leaked," he'll smile and respond, "Actually, it was on CDs." It's understandable why the police suspected him. He's a data-transparency revolutionary. In April 2009, two months before local elections, he posted a searchable database of Croatian voters, popisbiraca.pollitika.com, which also exposed widespread fraud. His purpose was to shine light on the fact that there are more people registered to vote in Croatia than are residents. In many cases, this is because people in neighboring Bosnia or Serbia are taking advantage of loose procedures in border towns in order to gain valuable social benefits, but Rakar points out that local authorities encourage the practice because it gives them an ample pool of extra votes to keep themselves in power.

Rakar says that Croatia is the only country in the world "where the number of voters exceeds the number of inhabitants." In one town, he found the suspicious address of "Dusina 0" (who lives at "zero"?) with 404 registered voters—

seventy-six percent of the town's total voter roll. By posting the whole list online in searchable form, he invited his fellow Croatians to investigate their own neighborhoods and towns, and to report the results back to his site, Pollitika.com. The resulting uproar was front-page news in Croatia for days, and has provoked a serious debate about amending the country's Constitution to make it illegal for citizens to be registered to vote in more than one country.

In a country of about two million Internet users, Pollitika has a huge footprint. Rakar started it in 2006 after his refusal to pay bribes to government tax auditors drove his successful printing business into bankruptcy. The site is similar to DailyKos, in that anyone can create an account and start blogging on it, but it is open to the whole political spectrum, with Rakar working to encourage civil debate. It now has 4,000 registered users (one-tenth of one percent of the country's adult population) and garners about 150,000 unique visitors each month.

"The whole point of Pollitika," Rakar tells me, "is to create a place where ordinary citizens can discuss politics. And there is a number of concerned citizens who wish to do so. Unlike DailyKos, it is open for both left and right sides, and if we start talking together, we will sooner or later find common ground and we can then build upon that."

Rakar earns very little from running Pollitika, though he says wryly, "to make government unhappy has its own rewards." Since he became a political blogger, he has also backed a few maverick candidates for office. In 2007, he ran the Social Democrats' online campaign; he backed Ivo Josipovic in his campaign for Croatia's (largely ceremonial) presidency; and more recently he helped an unknown candidate for mayor of Zagreb come from nowhere to grab forty percent of the vote against the incumbent. He is now looking to start a "serious citizen journalism site" that would offer analytical, behind-the-news reporting, blending citizen contributions with professional moderation.

I asked him why he does what he does. "It's hard to express," he says. "I just want to see a better country." But he is muckraking for a harder reason too: "Croatian history is full of 'unfinished' stories, and unless we start talking and resolving them we will be forever burdened by our past."

Rakar is just one of many small-d democratic activists turning to technology-powered transparency to drive change in their countries. In Kenya, lawyer Ory Okolloh created Mzalendo.com in 2006 to "keep an eye on the Kenyan Parliament." Like England's TheyWorkForYou.com and America's OpenCongress.org, Mzalendo got started because the official sources of information were woefully inadequate. Information on such basic questions as how an MP voted on a bill or what they said in a debate was almost impossible to obtain, let alone the details of how money was being spent. After Parliament voted itself a pay raise, Okolloh had had enough. "They were getting all this money, but we have no idea what they were doing to earn that money," she told the BBC News. "Parliament is not televised. The newspapers do a lousy job of covering it," she added.

In its early days, she and another blogger, known only as "M," had to go to Parliament and gather whatever information they could by hand, even memory. Note-taking from the public gallery without a press pass was not allowed. Other volunteers starting pitching in their own eyewitness accounts of debates. Eventually, MPs began contributing by sending corrections to their profiles, answering questions and joining in the debates on the site.[2] Their project was gaining its footing. But what happened next couldn't have been predicted by anyone: Okolloh and her network of friends hit upon an idea for documenting postelection problems in Kenya that has since stormed the world.

Okolloh, who had started a blog called KenyanPundit.com while a student at Harvard Law, found herself drawn into the center of a maelstrom in the aftermath of her country's December 2007 national elections. The election was rife with fraud, and while the incumbent President Mwai Kibaki claimed victory, violence broke out and tribal divisions threatened to tear the country apart. As things broke down, the government stopped all live broadcasting on radio and TV. Okolloh's blog became a hub of otherwise suppressed information, with Kenyan journalists and sources from inside the divided political parties all sending her updates. "The disconnect between what I was hearing from my sources and what was happening in the media was very wide," she recalls.

Late the night of January 3, 2008, Okolloh posted another update on her blog, full of what she was hearing from all her sources. Two paragraphs stood out:

Google Earth supposedly shows in great detail where the damage is being done on the ground. It occurs to me that it will be useful to keep a record of this, if one is thinking long-term. For the reconciliation process to occur at the local level the truth of what happened will first have to come out. Guys looking to do something—any techies out there willing to do a mashup of where the violence and destruction is occurring using Google Maps?

Speaking of documenting truth, it also occurs to me that we have no reliable figures of the real death tolls on the ground. Perhaps we can begin to collect information from organizations and individuals on the ground e.g. red cross, hospitals, etc. and start to build a tally online, preferably with names. Most of the people losing their lives will remain nameless, and it might be worthwhile to at least change that. Any volunteers/ideas?[3]

Halfway around the world in the United States, programmer Erik Hersman, who was already following Okolloh's blog closely, echoed her idea. "If there was ever a need for citizen journalism," he wrote on his own blog, WhiteAfrican.com, "then this is it."

Hersman also added a key insight into how Okolloh's

distributed reporting system could work: "The primary means of communication during an emergency in Kenya is via SMS —on their mobile phones."[4] Soon, he, developers David Kobia, Juliana Rotich, and other volunteer programmers were hard at work, or as Okolloh put it on January 7, "the Google mashup idea is cooking."[5] (One helpful precedent that was also on the team's mind: a Google Map of the refugee situation in Darfur that was sponsored by the U.S. Holocaust Memorial Museum.[6] The difference here, though, was to do reporting in real-time, not after the fact.)

Two days later, Okolloh's post announced: "Last week, in between nightmares about where my country was going, I was dreaming of a Google Mashup to document incidents of violence, looting etc. that have occurred during the post-election crisis. Today, Ushahidi is born." Named for the Swahili word for "witness," Ushahidi.com had a simple purpose, she explained:

> We believe that the number of deaths being reported by the government, police, and media is grossly underreported. We also don't think we have a true picture of what is really going on—reports that all have us have heard from family and friends in affected areas suggests that things are much worse than what we have heard in the media. We also (in my idealist world) hope that we can begin to put names and faces to the people who have lost their lives in this mess. What's the point of all this, you might ask? Well, Kenyans have demonstrated their capacity for selective amnesia time and time again. When this crisis comes to an end, we don't want what

happened to be swept under the rug in the name of "moving forward"—for us to truly move forward, the truth of what happened needs to be told—Ushahidi (www.ushahidi.com) is our small way of contributing to that.[7]

Dozens of bloggers inside and outside Kenya covered Ushahidi's launch.[8] In five days, they had 13,000 page views. In its first three months of existence, Ushahidi logged thousands of reports, which they diligently worked to verify with local nongovernmental groups, and ultimately counted about 45,000 unique users in Kenya.

As Hersman was quick to admit, what he and his fellow programmers built wasn't all that original. After the 2004 tsunami that ravaged much of South Asia, online activists like American Andy Carvin created sites like Tsunami-Info.org, using RSS feeds to aggregate information meant to help relief efforts. In 2005, an ad hoc collaboration of a number of data mavens, including Carvin and Ethan Zuckerman, David Geilhufe, Zack Rosen, and Jon Lebkowsky, rallied coders and other volunteers to build a "PeopleFinder" database to aggregate reports of missing and displaced persons, as well as the "Katrina Aftermath" blog,[9] to capture and highlight people's stories of the disaster.[10] In August of 2008, as Hurricane Gustav threatened the Gulf Coast, Carvin led five hundred volunteers in building a similar crisis relief site—only this time the hard work was done in advance.[11]

As time went on, people started to explore other ways of sharing real-time information for some social good. For example, in October of 2008, a group of volunteer bloggers and developers loosely affiliated with the Personal Democracy Forum blog I edit, techPresident.com, that included folks like Carvin and Dave Troy, the inventor of TwitterVision, Andrew Turner of Geocommons and social media maven Deanna Zandt, realized that the real-time web could help with efforts to guard against voting problems on election day. In three weeks, a simple blog post sketching out the idea by my colleagues Nancy Scola and Allison Fine led to a full-blown monitoring project called Twitter Vote Report.[12] Voters were encouraged to use Twitter, as well as other tools like iPhones, to share quick reports on the quality of their voting experience. Nearly 13,000 individual reports flowed in from more than 7,500 people. The result was a real-time picture of election-day complications and wait times that a number of journalistic organizations, including NPR, PBS, and several newspapers relied on for their reporting.[13] Some of Twitter Vote Report's underlying source code, which was written to enable volunteers to filter and add meta-data to raw user reports, actually went into a version of Ushahidi.[14]

But unlike all these other efforts, Ushahidi itself has gone on to power dozens of transparency projects, because the software itself is open source and designed to be relatively easy to customize for other projects. These include efforts to monitor elections in Bolivia, Brazil, Burundi, Colombia, Egypt, Ethiopia, Ghana, Guinea, Kyrgyzstan, India, Mexico, the Philippines, and Tanzania; to collect and display eyewitness reports during the 2008–09 Gaza War and the 2011 uprisings in Tunisia and Egypt; and to track pharmacy shortages in parts of East Africa. Ushahidi is so versatile as an open, crowd-based reporting tool it has even been used during blizzards in Washington, D.C., in 2009 and New York City in 2010 to help residents assist each other in cleaning up from their "snowmaggedons." In early 2011, the Australian Broadcasting Channel used it to crowd-map the impact of the Queensland flood.

And it has helped save lives. After the 2010 earthquake in Haiti, thousands of urgent reports were mapped on an Ushahidi-Haiti site that was set up in just two hours. Volunteers pitched in all over the world, including many from the Haitian diaspora, who helped with translating text messages from Creole. A representative of the Marine Corps, which was sent to Haiti to provide relief, told Ushahidi staff, "I cannot overemphasize to you what the work of the Ushahidi/Haiti has provided. It is saving lives every day. I wish I had time to document to you every example, but there are too many and our operation is moving too fast. . . . The Marine Corps is using your project every second of the day to get aid and assistance to the people that need it most."[15] Ushahidi's usefulness and versatility has attracted attention and support, including a prize from the Knight Foundation and a $1.4 million grant from the Omidyar Network.

Thousands of miles from each other, connected civic activists using inexpensive and readily available technology are building these kinds of collaborative democracy-opening projects. Here are short descriptions of some of my favorites:

- IPaidABribe.com is a project launched in August 2010 by a Bangalore, India–based nonprofit called Janaagraha that is trying to reduce rampant corruption there by inviting citizens to share their stories of either paying or resisting paying bribes to public officials. The idea is to provide a transparent view into the pattern of bribery occurring across a city, which Janaagraha will then use to push for improved governance and better law enforcement. While the site loads, you see an announcement—"240 departments in seventeen cities have been bribed"—and then a series of interactive charts invite you to discover where conditions are worst. The Bangalore transportation commissioner has already asked Janaagraha for a list of the complaints against his agency, leading to warnings to twenty senior officers. "The details about rampant corruption in my department are absolutely true," he told a local paper.[16]
- WikiCrimes.com is a collaborative crime-mapping

platform conceived by Professor Vasco Furtado of the University of Fortaleza, Brazil, to allow victims or witnesses of crimes to safely report that information on a searchable map. In some parts of the country, as many as half the crimes committed never get reported to police because citizens don't believe the cops will act; as a result, official police statistics undercount the actual crime rates. By breaking the authorities' monopoly on crime information and making relevant data more transparent, WikiCrimes hopes to force real reforms in Brazil's criminal justice system. "The idea is very simple," Furtado says. "When people are robbed, it's quite common for them to tell other people. With WikiCrimes this information will be available globally."[17]

- SeeClickFix.com is an American start-up launched by Ben Berkowitz, a native of New Haven, who wanted a way to ensure that when he reported to the city that some graffiti needed cleaning, his complaint didn't disappear down a bureaucratic black hole. The site—which is similar in some ways to mySociety's FixMyStreet—enables anyone with a phone or a web connection to report nonemergency issues in their communities, which get placed on a local map with a time stamp and room for comments. The reports are transparent and searchable online, which gives everyone—neighborhood groups, elected officials, and government service providers—the ability to see what issues are festering, thus creating an incentive to resolve them more effectively. SeeClickFix is actually a for-profit company with some four hundred paying clients, including cities like Tuscon, Arizona, and Washington, D.C., that embed the tool on their websites and plug its reports into their municipal systems. More than 60,000 user-generated reports have been registered on the site since its founding in 2008. (See also "It's Buggered Mate," a somewhat cheeky Australian version of the same idea.)

The Technology for Transparency Network (TTN) has documented close to sixty examples of efforts using online and/or mobile tools to promote transparency and accountability, from Argentina to Zimbabwe.[18] They range from Cambodia's Sithi.org, which is a human rights portal that is working to collect reports of human rights violations, to sophisticated and reasonably well-staffed operations like Chile's Vota Intelligente, which offers a range of transparency and participation tools modeled on sites like mySociety's TheyWorkForYou and FixMyStreet, and OpenCongress in the United States.

Not every transparency project is centered on high-tech; often activists find ingenious ways to blend high- and low-tech to expand public access to vital information. In

India, for example, there has been a long struggle to get the government to abolish the colonial-era Official Secrets Act, which culminated with the 2005 passage of a critical "Right to Information" law that allows any citizen to request and receive government documents. This has turned into a powerful tool for poor people to expose local corruption. Now that the government has begun posting detailed reporting of anti-poverty spending online, activists with the "Right to Information" movement have developed ingenious ways to insure that poor villagers that lack web access can find out where the money is supposedly going. Their solution merges high-technology with the most basic of simple tools: a paint-brush. All over India's rural villages, "Transparency Walls" are being painted at popular gathering places, displaying the government's spending spreadsheets in analog form. In the state of Rajastan alone, more than 100,000 of these vivid displays can be found. Villagers then conduct "social audits," literally going door-to-door with the employment data, talking to workers and checking its accuracy.[19]

In addition to all of these country-specific projects, there are a handful of multinational efforts underway worth noting. For example, building on the pioneering work of the Environmental Working Group in the United States in opening up information on agriculture subsidies, activists with a group called EUTransparency.org starting pushing for access to farm-subsidy data from their own governments.

Their site, FarmSubsidy.org, aggregates information from twenty-seven European Union countries that have released their data—more than 181 billion euros in payments to more than twenty million recipients. Or take UNDemocracy.com, an effort by a British programmer named Julian Todd that makes all the proceedings of the United Nations General Assembly, Security Council, and various agencies available in Web 2.0–compliant form. As Todd says on the site's home page, "this project is a hobby begun by volunteers who recognized that the accessibility of these vital documents was so limited they had to do something about it themselves, since there was no evidence it was going to happen by itself."

As these projects proliferate, a community of practice is steadily evolving with some common understandings about how best to work together. First, there is an emerging consensus on the need for open data and common standards. In December 2007, I was privileged to be one of thirty open government advocates who gathered in Sebastopol, California, for a meeting hosted by Carl Malamud and Tim O'Reilly to develop a set of principles for "open government data." Our group, which included Josh Tauberer of GovTrack.us, Tom Steinberg of mySociety.org, David Moore and Donny Shaw of OpenCongress.org, Ethan Zuckerman of the Berkman Center, and Lawrence Lessig (then at Stanford), came up with a simple declaration of eight core principles. The technical details are in a footnote—what matters more is how we articulated the value of open data itself:[20]

> The Internet is the public space of the modern world, and through it governments now have the opportunity to better understand the needs of their citizens and citizens may participate more fully in their government. Information becomes more valuable as it is shared, less valuable as it is hoarded. Open data promotes increased civil discourse, improved public welfare, and a more efficient use of public resources.

In this understanding, the relationship between governments and their constituents is a two-way street, and data is the road that connects them. The more granular, accurate, and open that data, the more timely and accessible, and the freer the access to it, the broader the connection and the better the results.

Common open standards also mean ensuring that we share data using formats that allow for easy comparison and joining of databases and web services. To use a non-technical metaphor: if one hundred fifty years ago every city in America had built its rail lines on radically different gauges, train manufacturers could never have standardized production. Today, transparency advocates are pushing government bodies to adopt interoperable formats for structuring different kinds of public data. That way, if one city shares its crime location reports and an app developer builds a program that shows you where it's safe to walk home at night, the app could work on other cities' data as it gets released.[21]

A third important understanding that transparency advocates have learned from hard experience: when involving the public, keep it simple. Don't expect many volunteers to do intrinsically hard tasks. Reporting an incident at a polling place or coding an earmark request is relatively easy. Investigating whether that incident actually involved planned political intimidation, or figuring out if a particular earmark is tied to a campaign contributor, is much harder. Colleagues at the Sunlight Foundation learned this lesson by experience. Early on, they published a list of earmarks in a big transportation bill and set up a search tool that would give users a list of earmarks in their zip code. Users were asked to then try to figure out if the recipient and their member of Congress had any corrupting entanglements. Even though there were thousands of examples, only a few people managed to uncover anything of consequence—the task was too hard and too diffuse for a crowd-scouring project.

A few months later, Bill Allison, the head of Sunlight's Reporting Group, had a different brainstorm. Why not ask volunteers to help investigate how many members paid their spouses or children money from campaign funds? While this is a completely legal practice, it is also the method by which disgraced Congressman Tom DeLay of Texas funneled hundreds of thousands of dollars from campaign contributors into his family's pocket. The "Is Congress a Family Business?" project broke the task down into two steps: visitors to the website were given a choice of members to look up, then guided first to one public resource where they could look up the names of family members, and then from there to the OpenSecrets.org page for that members' campaign expenditures. If they found a match between a spouse's name and a campaign expense, they were prompted to punch in the total. Finishing the process, the website thanked each user, gave an update—so far, XX members have been found who have paid $YY to their family—and asked a tempting question: Would you like to investigate another?

The project launched on a Friday afternoon of a holiday weekend. By Sunday, volunteers had finished the work. One person had looked up more than a hundred members of Congress on his own. Why? "It was addictive, like eating potato chips," he told the Sunlight staff. "I couldn't do just one." Sunlight's staff double-checked the matches and then reported that nineteen members of Congress had spouses on their campaign payrolls making more than $600,000. The Internet is great for involving large numbers of volunteers in the easier tasks; the harder ones still require skilled workers.

Finally, the last thing all these projects tend to embrace is their own transparency, by publishing detailed lists of their funding and sharing lots of information about how they're developing projects, not just the results. By blogging with open comments and developing policy on open email lists, groups have discovered again and again the power of open networks.

Trying to solve a problem within your own small network of co-workers and colleagues is usually harder than opening it up to the wisdom of a larger crowd. Had Ory Okolloh not been blogging in such an engaging way, for example, all the people who cared about Kenya's future probably wouldn't have been commenting on her posts, and the serendipitous connections that developed between her, Erik Hersman, and the rest of the early Ushahidi developer team might not have happened.

All these developments haven't gone unnoticed by politicians or government officials. As the transparency movement has grown, establishments have started to respond with everything from lip service to real action. In the last few years in both the United States and United Kingdom, the major political parties have started to compete against each other to be seen as the most committed to openness in government. But as we shall see, the rhetoric is much richer than the reality.

6

Open Government:
A Movement or a Mirage?

People tend not to trust what is hidden. Transparency is a powerful tool to demonstrate to the public that the government is spending our money wisely, that politicians are not in the pocket of lobbyists and special-interest groups, that government is operating in an accountable manner, and that decisions are made to ensure the safety and protection of all Americans.

—"Moving Toward a 21st Century Right-to-Know Agenda," Recommendations from the Right-to-Know Community to the Obama-Biden Transition, November 2008

On January 21, 2009, his first full day in office, Barack Obama issued a presidential memorandum on "transparency and open government." Many observers, including me, expressed hope that Obama's words would actually signal the most important shift in how government works in America since the rise of the New Deal. In five succinct paragraphs, he promised to create an "unprecedented level of openness in Government." "We will work together to ensure the public trust and establish a system of transparency, public participation, and collaboration," he wrote, arguing that it would "strengthen our democracy and promote efficiency and effectiveness in Government."

In addition to making government more transparent, he also declared that it should become more participatory and collaborative:

> Public engagement enhances the Government's effectiveness and improves the quality of its decisions. Knowledge is widely dispersed in society, and public officials benefit from having access to that dispersed knowledge. Executive departments and agencies should offer Americans increased opportunities to participate in policymaking and to provide their Government with the benefits of their collective expertise and information. . . . Executive departments and agencies should use innovative tools, methods, and systems to cooperate among themselves, across all levels of Government, and with nonprofit organizations, businesses, and individuals in the private sector.[1]

Simultaneously, he put out a second presidential memorandum on the Freedom of Information Act, reversing the Bush Administration's eight-year policy of withholding as much information as possible from the public. "The Freedom of Information Act should be administered with a clear presumption: In the face of doubt, openness prevails. The Government should not keep information confidential merely because public officials might be embarrassed by disclosure, because errors and failures might be revealed, or because of speculative or abstract fears. . . . The presumption of disclosure also means that agencies should take affirmative steps to make information public. They should not wait for specific requests from the public. All agencies should use modern technology to inform citizens about what is known and done by their Government. Disclosure should be timely."[2]

The language was dry but the message was clear: by emphasizing open, participatory, and collaborative government, Obama was pointing toward a third way between the stale left-right dichotomy of "big government" versus "smaller government." Effective government, Obama was suggesting, could be found by opening up the bureaucracy to direct public monitoring, engagement, and, where viable, collaboration.

Obama's call for more transparency in government mirrored earlier statements made by Democratic leaders when they retook control of Congress in 2006. "The Democrats intend to lead the most honest, most open and most ethical Congress in history," incoming House Speaker Nancy Pelosi said the night of the 2006 election when her ascension became apparent.[3] Some significant steps were taken, including the imposition of tougher limits on accepting gifts and travel paid for by outside groups, quarterly reports by lobbyists (instead of biannual ones), online posting of earmark requests, and electronic filing of financial disclosure statements and lobbyist reports.

Pelosi and her Republican counterpart, Rep. John

Boehner, also announced that they were interested in improving how the House of Representatives made use of the Internet. In response the Sunlight Foundation set up the "Open House Project," chaired by two Democratic and two Republican activists, to develop a set of recommendations, which I played a small role in.[4] Ultimately the House implemented several of the project's key recommendations, including creating permanent links to legislative documents on Thomas and posting feeds from some congressional committees' websites. Perhaps the biggest change the project succeeded in winning was a wholesale update in Congressional franking rules, to now allow members to communicate directly with their constituents using modern multimedia tools like Twitter, YouTube, and Facebook.[5]

But the unfortunate truth is that when it comes to core issues of transparency, participation, and collaboration, not that much has changed in how either the White House or Congress actually behaves. Some government agencies are genuinely innovating, and the same can be said for a handful of politicians and government bodies outside the Beltway. But so far, enacting real transparency for how Washington works remains an orphan issue—politicians coo at the baby but no one, other than a few outsiders, really wants to adopt it.

Take Obama, for starters. During the transition process between the election and his actually taking office, his official website, Change.gov, hosted several open discussions. Over the course of two rounds, more than 120,000 people voted nearly 6 million times on more than 85,000 questions that were posted. In both cases, top administration officials offered answers to a handful of the top-voted issues. They also invited the public to contribute to a "Citizens' Briefing Book," an attempt to make sure that at least some iconoclastic ideas from ordinary people made their way unfiltered directly into the president's hands. More than 125,000 people voted on more than 44,000 submissions, and several months later, the White House Office of Public Engagement released a thirty-two-page PDF along with a video showing Obama holding the report.

Twice, in the first six months of his administration, Obama held an interactive "online town hall" where the public was invited to submit questions in advance and the President responded during a live webcast done in tandem with an in-the-flesh town-hall meeting. First, in late March, his new media team held an online town hall about the economy. For two days, anyone could post a question on the White House website or vote one to the top of the pile. Then Obama held a live webcast from the White House where he pointedly responded to most of the top-voted questions. Nearly 93,000 people submitted more than 100,000 questions, and more than 3.6 million votes were cast on them. Tens of thousands watched the event live online. The forum was generally deemed a success, but it hit one discordant note when Obama made fun of the fact that questions about legalizing marijuana did surprisingly well in the online voting. "I don't know what this says about the online audience," he chuckled, ignoring the fact that somewhere between forty and fifty percent of American voters favor the reform.

Then, in early July, the president held another online town hall on health care reform, but despite using sites like YouTube, Facebook, and Twitter to invite the submissions of questions from the public, this event was far less interactive than his first. Obama said he'd answer some of the "more popular" questions, but there was no mechanism established to determine which ones were indeed popular. Instead, his staff chose which questions he would be asked to respond to, producing an event that was less spontaneous and less town-hall-like than if all the questions had come from citizens live at the event using no technology at all. Reporters at the daily White House briefing peppered press secretary Robert Gibbs with critical questions about the event, attacking it as a sham. My colleague at the Sunlight Foundation, Ellen Miller, called it "transparency theater," though the more precise term might be "participation theater."

That said, initially there were good reasons to believe that Obama understood how operating government in a more transparent and interactive way could help restore trust in government, and thus strengthen his ability to implement other goals. Early in his administration, Obama made several declarations about how his approach to government, and in particular the giant $787 billion "Economic Recovery" spending plan that was the major legislative priority of his first months in office, would be informed by direct public participation in the process. In one online video, he told his supporters that this program would be conducted "with unprecedented transparency and accountability." Clearly aware that his critics were already predicting "big government" would waste hundreds of billions in taxpayer dollars, he added:

> I'll appoint an aggressive Inspector General and a cabinet-level oversight board to make sure your money is spent wisely. More importantly, I'll enlist all of you. As soon as this plan is signed into law, Recovery.gov goes live and you'll be able to see precisely where your tax dollars are going. Because this is your democracy, and as I said throughout the campaign, change never begins from the top down. It begins from the bottom up.[6]

A day later, on February 9, 2009, selling his recovery plan at a town-hall meeting in economically devastated Elkhart, Indiana, he went further in explaining his vision for using the social web to involve the public in the watchdogging of government spending:

> We're actually going to set up something called Recovery.gov—this is going to be a special website we set up, that gives you a report on where the money is going in your community, how it's being spent, how many jobs it's created so that all of you can be the eyes and ears. And if you see that a project is not working the way it's supposed to,

you'll be able to get on that website and say, "You know, I thought this was supposed to be going to school construction but I haven't noticed any changes being made." And that will help us track how this money is being spent. . . . The key is that we're going to have strong oversight and strong transparency to make sure this money isn't being wasted.[7]

"I'll enlist all of you." "You can be the eyes and ears." These sounded like the words of someone who clearly understood the power and wisdom of a crowd, and the axiom that all of us are smarter than any one of us.

But here's what actually happened with Recovery.gov. Earl Devaney, a former Secret Service agent who was appointed as the inspector general to run the stimulus program's Recovery and Transparency Accountability Board, promised that the site would invite Americans to be "citizens inspectors general," helping track whether the money was indeed being used properly. "The website will unleash a million citizen IGs [inspectors general]," Devaney said in August 2009. "After getting a taste of this, people will not want to go back to the old ways," he said.[8]

No such thing has happened. First of all, the Recovery.gov site doesn't really engage the public as "eyes and ears" apart from offering a way for people to report fraud, waste, or abuse via a standard electronic complaint form. In other words, all the real information processing about possible problems with government spending is hidden from the public; people have no way of seeing each other's complaints or tracking whether something has been addressed. All the real work is done by a sophisticated "Recovery Operations Center" where traditional law enforcement authorities use data-mining tools to uncover potential fraud. In no way has a community of citizen inspectors general been formed, and it's not surprising that Recovery.gov has had no discernible effect on public trust in Obama.

Over on Inspector General Devaney's "Chairman's Corner" blog, a handful of posts (less than one per month!) demonstrate further how out of touch he is with how to engage the social web. In his March 2010 post, he lambasted "gratuitous criticism from some journalists and Internet grouches"[9] who pointed out problems with Recovery.gov's public data, instead of embracing their comments as constructive. My colleague Clay Johnson, then director of Sunlight Labs, chided Devaney for how poorly he dealt with online criticism, writing: "You could have created a spirit of civil openness and participation like no other in an incredibly charged political environment. You could have been a textbook model for every federal agency as they are writing their open government plans. . . . But instead you decided to go on the defensive. You decided to belittle the participants, and to further the controversy. You decided to keep up the data hysteria and draw a wall around yourself."[10] Seven months later—and more than a year into Recovery.gov's operation—Devaney announced the launch of a public-facing blog which he said was "meant to give you a voice in what we're doing [and be] a forum for your thoughts, comments and suggestions."[11] In its first four months of operation, from October 2010 to this writing, the blog received about ten comments per month from the public. So much for Obama's promise to enlist ordinary people in making government more efficient.

While the White House itself has done little to build on Obama's glowing rhetoric beyond posting online the records of visitors to the building, at the agency level there have been some meaningful changes. A year after issuing a detailed "Open Government Directive," several agencies, including the Department of Labor, Health and Human Services, and NASA, genuinely began sharing significant internal data with the public. By contrast, observed John Wonderlich, the policy director of the Sunlight Foundation, "If you look at the Department of Defense . . . the Open Government Plan they released . . . was really, for the most part, boiler plate language and plans to make plans about other plans and to set up a new commission that will report to another commission."[12]

On Data.gov, the administration's new flagship central repository for open data, you can download chemical exposure health data, work-related injury data, mine safety data, Medicare cost data, air quality records, and thousands of other interesting data sets. You can even rate databases and sort by other users' ratings, a rough way of discovering some of the most interesting resources. Third-party developers have begun building applications using some of this data, another positive sign. On IT.UsaSpending.gov, Vivek Kundra, the administration's chief information officer, offers a cutting-edge look into the details of agency technology spending, complete with transparent ratings of hundreds of projects. And a long list of agencies have started using YouTube, Facebook, MySpace, and dozens of less well-known but equally potent Web 2.0 platforms, thanks to efforts by the White House new media team and the Government Accountability Office to negotiate acceptable terms of service with these third-party services. More than one hundred agencies now have official Twitter accounts, for example.

Unfortunately, usage of social media tools like Twitter and Facebook have come to be seen as proof that government officials and politicians have embraced the networked age, when in fact most of the time they are still just talking *at* their constituents rather than *with* them. Two recent studies by the Congressional Research Service looked at Twitter use by members of the House and Senate and found that a plurality of their tweets were of the press release variety. Only a tiny percentage of these replies were actually addressed to other Twitter users.[13] Just a handful of politicians use social media as adeptly as Cory Booker, the mayor of Newark, New Jersey, who has more than a million followers online and is constantly engaged in two-way communication with his constituents—to the point of showing up personally to shovel driveways and deliver diapers to snowbound families after receiving tweets during a blizzard.

In years of tracking the impact of two-way technology on politics, I have only encountered a handful of substantive breaks from this pattern of top-down behavior. In 2007, the U.S. Patent and Trademark Office launched the "Peer-to-Patent" experiment, which had been midwifed into existence by Beth Noveck, then a professor at New York Law School. Faced with a huge backlog of patents awaiting review, the "Peer-to-Patent" program invited members of the public to assist in a key step in the process by looking for examples of "prior art." Patent examiners then use the findings to decide if an invention is actually original or a knockoff. Through a well-structured website, PtP attracted thousands of helpful hands, or, as Noveck put it, "rather than going to the experts, the USPTO realized that it is easier to let the experts find it."[14] In two years, more than 2,800 people signed up to be reviewers. And the vast majority of patent examiners found their work to be helpful and told evaluators they wanted the experiment implemented as a regular practice. Peer-to-Patent's success as a pilot project propelled Noveck into the White House under Obama, where she pushed with varying degrees of success to implement similar ideas across government. (More on her role below.)

In 2007, Steve Urquhart, the Republican chairman of the Utah House of Representatives Rules Committee, launched a wiki called Politicopia, where he promised to post the text of pending legislation before his committee and invited the public in to comment. Thousands of people did, and Urquhart credits the dialogue that resulted in affecting the outcome on several pending bills, including one on school vouchers and another on abortion. Commenting on the passage of the voucher legislation, Urquhart said, "For six years we've been chasing our tail on this bill, and today the bill passed in very large part because of Politicopia." He explained how: "When private dialogue was made public, the main area of criticism was publicly revealed to be fictitious."[15]

Another valuable experiment that also happened in 2007 was something called "Legislation 2.0." Richard Durbin, a top Democratic leader in U.S. Senate, decided to turn to political blogs on the left and right for advice on crafting a national broadband bill. And he didn't do this in an offhand way—a staffer worked on the project in advance, to line up participation from a variety of industry and public interest representatives and to get buy-in from blogs like OpenLeft and RedState, top hubs respectively for Democratic and Republican conversation. "I think this is a unique experiment in transparent government and an opportunity to demonstrate the democratic power of the Internet," Durbin said as he kicked off the project. "If we're successful, it could become a model for the way legislation on health care, foreign policy, and education is drafted in the future."[16] Over the course of several days, Durbin and his staff blogged and responded to comments in the threads that developed. He promised to draft legislative language and post that online for further comment.

Other sitting legislators have ventured into similar territory. For example, Senator Claire McCaskill asked the public for suggestions to help her prioritize what hearings she should hold as chair of the subcommittee on contracting oversight. More than 600 people voted on 228 suggestions, using the Google Moderator tool for sorting through the pool.[17] More recently, House Republicans launched a participatory project called YouCut, which invited voters to go through a list of possible spending cuts each week, with a promise to put each top-voted choice to a vote. Over the first thirteen weeks of the experiment, they tallied more than 75,000 suggestions for cuts and collected more than 1.3 million votes from the public.[18] And starting in 2009, the New York State Senate began accepting online public comments on all bills,[19] with some of them receiving more than 100 comments. A new service, BillBuzz, even allows senators, staffers, and the public to subscribe to daily updates showing comments on particular bills or on those sponsored by a particular lawmaker.[20]

And the Obama administration hasn't given up completely on trying, at least at the agency level, to open up to more two-way dialogue using interactive media. Late in 2009, Sudan Special Envoy Scott Gration and Samantha Power, NSC Senior Director for Multilateral Affairs, sat down at the White House with the leaders of the largest, most vocal advocacy groups on Darfur issue, Jerry Fowler of Save Darfur and Layla Amjadi, the student director of STAND (the student-led division of the Genocide Intervention Network). The meeting was streamed live onto the web on not only the White House and State Department websites, but also on the Save Darfur and STAND sites, making it an unusually open meeting, especially considering both advocacy groups have often been tough critics of the administration. Imagine the Treasury Department holding a public forum with Public Citizen and the Campaign for America's Future on banking policy, for example, or the Agriculture Department doing something similar with the Sierra Club. Both groups were able to canvass their memberships to submit and/or select questions in advance to ask Gration and Power. It was a moment where outside advocacy group leaders really had a chance to put administration decision makers on the spot and ask tough questions, where the web was included as a way to amplify a dialogue, not just a monologue from above. Alas, it has not been repeated.

As Obama's White House deputy chief technology officer for open government, Beth Noveck also worked hard to build on the principles of transparency, participation and collaboration that Obama had embraced, and her fingerprints can be found on the open data portals and projects like Data.gov. Thanks to her efforts, every government agency is now authorized to use the brainstorming tool Ideascale to invite public input in a more open way than merely collecting comments. And though she left her post midway through Obama's first term, she also planted the seeds for the creation of more sophisticated tools for creating and managing useful citizen consultations, including one called "ExpertNet" that certainly bears watching. But as she noted in a January 2011 personal blog post after returning to civilian life, "At present, there is no opportunity for people outside of government to propose a prize-backed challenge, public-private partnership, social behavioral 'nudge,' collective volunteer action, or new software platform as complements or alternatives to create the desired behavior change and consumer protection. . . . In order to enjoy 'a 21st century government that's open and competent,' as the President said last night [at the State of the Union address], we need to network government—not reorg it."[21]

The new Republican leadership of the House of Representatives has promised to make their proceedings much more open than their predecessors, but it is too soon to say what will come of their promises. If all goes as claimed, bills will be posted online in a searchable format three days prior to a vote, bill markups will be announced three days in advance, formal committee votes and amendments will be fully disclosed, and hearings will be webcast and archived for later access.[22] These changes would make it markedly easier to monitor Congress's work. But we still won't know what members of Congress are doing when they meet with lobbyists, nor will we know anything but the roughest range of their personal financial holdings in companies whose business they may oversee.

Transparency and participatory politics has run through a similarly checkered path in the United Kingdom in recent years. For a time, it appeared that the U.K.'s Labour government was inching close to embracing a much more people-driven vision of open government, akin to Obama's "eyes and ears" notion of crowd-sourcing. First, in early 2007, the prime minister's office (then under Tony Blair) hired mySociety.org to build a tool enabling the public to create and sign petitions to his office directly from the 10 Downing Street website.[23] Millions of citizens swarmed in, and some of the top petitions forced the government to make actual policy changes, like dropping plans for a new vehicle tax. Tom Steinberg of mySociety was then asked to coauthor a study along with Ed Mayo, the head of the National Consumer Council, on the "power of information" to foster new kinds of citizen-to-citizen information sharing and collaboration. They recommended a strategy in which government:

- welcomes and engages with users and operators of

user-generated sites in pursuit of common social and economic objectives;

- supplies innovators that are re-using government-held information with the information they need, when they need it, in a way that maximizes the long-term benefits for all citizens; and

- protects the public interest by preparing citizens for a world of plentiful (and sometimes unreliable) information, and helps excluded groups take advantage.[24]

Cabinet Minister Tom Watson—whose formal title was "Minister for Transformational Government"—was an enthusiastic proponent of Steinberg and Mayo's report. An early convert to blogging, he had personal experience as a politician who actually understood how opening oneself up to a transparent dialogue with one's constituents can improve government in many ways. A year after the launch of the prime minister's e-petition platform, Watson was thinking ahead in radical terms: "Over seven million electronic signatures have been sent, electronically, to the Downing Street petition website," he noted in a speech about the power of information. "One in ten citizens have emailed the Prime Minister about an issue. The next stage is to enable e-petitioners to connect with each other around particular issues and to link up with policy debates both on and off Government web space." Watson gave a wonderfully illustrative example of how this could work with other government websites that attract lots of traffic from the public:

> I recently registered my local Labour Party with groupsnearyou.com. This is a new site provided by the MySociety people. It's a site for people who run small-scale community focused groups. Through the site, I found West Bromwich Freecycle. I'm the Member of Parliament for West Bromwich East and I didn't know about an important recycling initiative going on in my own patch. This information now means that a bag load of clothing for a small child and a habitat sofa are about given a second chance to give pleasure.
>
> A simple, free tool enabled a small social good. Do this on at scale and you have a very good thing going on. Nine million people now pay their car tax online. Wouldn't it be great if when they have finished their transaction they can be directed to a kind of golden page that lets them find small local community groups in their area or offers them a menu of things to do that are good. Recycling one sofa is one thing. Recycling nine million sofas is a big contribution to sustainable communities.[25]

This idea of transparent government acting as a convener of citizens around common public goods has yet to happen in Britain. In February 2009 the Labour government started a modest experiment called "Show Us a Better Way," which was a £20,000 contest that encouraged the public to submit ideas on how to improve the way public data was made available online. But little more came of it, as the government was running out of steam on other fronts and politicians like Watson were caught up in Labour Party infighting as the Parliament expenses scandal broke and general elections approached. The idea of government websites enabling public collaboration is also probably still ahead of its time. As Steinberg noted in the wake of his work for the Labour government, "If the government said that people can't drive on the roads to go to a rally to protest something, because it would lead to bad press, everyone would protest. Yet when government says that it can't let people using government websites connect to each other, in order to challenge the status quo, no one says anything."[26] Someday, this will change.

The one change that did make it through the British political system these last few years mirrors the positive moves fostered by Obama's open government initiative: the creation of Data.gov.uk as a central repository for releasing and promoting the use of open data. In response to the expenses scandal, then–Prime Minister Gordon Brown announced that he had appointed Sir Tim Berners-Lee, the father of the World Wide Web, to "help us drive the opening up of access to government data in the web."[27] It didn't hurt that Berners-Lee brought real star power to the issue. As James Crabtree and Tom Chatfield reported in an in-depth cover story cheekily titled "Mash the State" for *Prospect* magazine, cabinet ministers were more interested in meeting him than the other way around. "When faced with Berners-Lee's demands, ministers usually said yes," he recounts.[28]

Like the new Republican House leadership in Washington, the new Conservative–Liberal Democratic coalition government has promised improvements in how the British government shares information with the public, pledging to release "a tsunami of data." The exact salaries of top officials have been made public, as well as the formal organizational chart for the Cabinet Office, something that no previous government had ever done. Gifts and travel benefits received by cabinet ministers will also be made public, and a quarterly report of which outside groups ministers have met with will also be published, a first step towards revealing who is lobbying the government for what. And the new government has kept its promise to start revealing the details of all government contracts worth more than £25,000.[29]

In general, the response of incumbents to the kind of transparency that causes them to lose power can be summed up nicely by the comments of a former president of the American League of Lobbyists. After hearing about the Sunlight Foundation's PublicMarkup.org site, which involved the public in drafting a model omnibus transparency bill, he told a reporter, "I don't think the way you advocate is to put everything online and say, 'All right American people, weigh in on that,' because then what's next? Are we going to let the American people decide our defense policy, our trade policy, our immigration policy?"[30]

Or consider the story of a website that never formally

saw the light of day, ChicagoWorksForYou.com. In June 2005, a team of developers working for the City of Chicago began developing a website that would take fifty-five different service requests that flow into the city's 311 database—items like pothole repairs, tree-trimming, garbage can placement, building permits, and restaurant inspections—and enable users to search by address and "map what's happening in your neighborhood." The idea was to showcase city services at the local level. A developer who worked on the project told me, "They were interested in showing community leaders how much they were doing for them." The site also included tracking data, such as "every single pothole that's been reported but hasn't yet been filled, for example."

ChicagoWorksForYou.com was finished in January 2006, with the full support of Mayor Richard Daley's office. But before it could be launched, it needed to be reviewed by the city's aldermen. According to my source, "they were very impressed with its functionality, but they were shocked at the possibility that it would go public." Aldermanic elections were coming up. "The aldermen were not interested in showing any service requests that were not filled, so as to deny their opponents in the upcoming elections any fodder for attacking them." So even if the site showed ninety percent of potholes being filled within thirty days, the powers that be didn't want the public to know about the last ten percent. ChicagoWorksForYou.com was shelved—

though you can view screenshots of it at that URL, preserved by one of the developers who worked on it and was miffed at its death.

But the idea of a website that brings together everything there is to be known about city services in Chicago is alive and kicking. If you go to EveryBlock.com, a site that was launched in July 2007, and click on their Chicago link, you can drill down to any ward, neighborhood or block and discover everything from the latest restaurant inspection reports and building permits to recent crime reports and street closures. It's all on an interactive map, and if you want to subscribe to updates about a particular location and type of report, the site kicks out all kinds of custom RSS feeds. Says Daniel O'Neill, one of EveryBlock's data mavens, "Crime and restaurant inspections are our hottest topics: will I be killed today and will I vomit today?"

EveryBlock now covers sixteen of America's largest cities, including New York, San Francisco, and Washington, D.C., offering one glimpse of the future of ubiquitous and hyperlocal information. EveryBlock's team started out by collecting most of their information by scraping it off of public websites and spreadsheets and turning it into structured data that can be easily displayed and manipulated online. But some cities, like Washington, have begun making their own public reports available directly in structured form.

Since 2006, all the raw data the District of Columbia

has collected on government operations, education, health care, crime, and dozens of other topics has been available for free to the public via 260 live data feeds. The city's CapStat online service also allows anyone to track the performance of individual agencies, monitor neighborhood issues, and make suggestions for improvement. Vivek Kundra, who was then D.C.'s innovative Chief Technology Officer (before becoming the Obama administration's first Chief Information Officer), called this "building the digital public square." In mid-October 2008, he announced an "Apps for Democracy" contest that offered $20,000 in cash prizes for outside developers and designers for web applications and tools that made useful visualizations from the city's data catalog.

In just a few weeks, Kundra received nearly fifty applications. The winners included:

- iLive.at, a site that shows with one click all the local information around one address, including the closest places to go shopping, buy gas, or mail a letter; the locations of recently reported crimes; and the demographic makeup of the local neighborhood;
- Where's My Money DC, a tool that meshes with Facebook and enables users to look up and discuss all city expenditures above $2,500; and
- Stumble Safely, an online guide to the best bars and safe paths to stumble home after a night out.

Had Kundra tried to get contractors to build a similar suite of websites for the city through the normal procurement process, he estimates it would have taken at least two years and cost the city millions of dollars. The lesson of the "Apps for Democracy" contest is simple: there is now a critical mass of citizens with the skills and the appetite to engage with public agencies in co-creating a new kind of self-government. If you give people greater access to public data, they will come up with all sorts of creative and useful ways of using it.[31]

Some thoughtful participants in the Internet politics arena have raised questions about pressing transparency as a strategy for political reform. Most notably, Harvard professor Lawrence Lessig, a longtime leader of the open culture movement, wrote a cover essay in October 2009 in *The New Republic* titled "Against Transparency: The Perils of Openness in Government." His worry was that the generic push to liberate government data, which he called "the naked transparency movement," would have the unintended consequence of worsening public understanding of the influences affecting lawmakers. "We are not thinking critically enough about where and when transparency works, and where and when it may lead to confusion, or to worse," he wrote. "And I fear that the inevitable success of this movement—if pursued alone, without any sensitivity to the full complexity of the idea of perfect openness—will inspire not reform, but disgust. The 'naked transparency movement,' as I will call it here, is not going to inspire change. It will simply push any faith in our political system over the cliff."

In Lessig's view, "naked transparency" will reinforce an already cynical culture's judgments about public officials:

> As Congress complies with the clear demands of transparency, and as coders devise better and more efficient ways to mash-up the data that Congress provides, we will see a future more and more inundated with claims about the links between money and results. Every step will have a plausible tie to troubling influence. Every tie will be reported. We will know everything there is to know about at least the publicly recordable events that might be influencing those who regulate us. The panopticon will have been turned upon the rulers.[32]

These are not unfair concerns. No one wants to make it even harder for people to go into public life. The "gotcha" school of journalism helps create a rigid culture inside government; if any small failure can be magnified out of proportion, best not to take any risks or do anything that might be innovative.

However, we can't restore much trust in government representatives by hiding more of what they do, or who tries to influence them, or by shoring up their power to arbitrarily hide information from the public. Increased transparency is a necessary condition for the revival of trust. Nor is anyone in the transparency movement arguing that raw government data alone is all we need. Context, stories, narrative, and analysis are all vital too—plus engaged citizens. Often, greater transparency can have the effect of helping citizens understand the many positive things that government does. For example, when activists started posting the details of congressional earmarks, many people were surprised and reassured to see how many of them went to credible and valuable projects, like funding for dialysis programs to keep diabetics from needing expensive emergency room services. Similarly, when Cablegate broke, a number of pundits commented on how often the cables showed American diplomats in a positive light.

The good news is, the day is not far off when it will be possible to see, at a glance, all of the most significant ways an individual, lobbyist, corporation, or interest group is influencing and benefiting from the political process in America, and all the ways an elected official, candidate, or government official may be affected by those influences. "If I search for Exxon, I want one-click disclosure," my friend Ellen Miller of the Sunlight Foundation says to me. "I want to see who its PAC is giving money to, who its executives and employees are supporting at the state and federal levels; who does its lobbying, whom they're meeting with, and what they're lobbying on; whether it is employing former government officials, or vice versa, if any of its ex-employees are in government; whether any of those people have flown on the company's jets; and then I also want to know what contracts, grants, or earmarks the company has gotten and whether they were competitively bid for."

She continues: "If I look up a senator, I want an up-to-date list of his campaign contributors—not one that is months out of date because the Senate still files those reports on paper. I want to see his public calendar of meetings, I want to know what earmarks he's sponsored and obtained, I want to know whether he is connected to a private charity that people might be funneling money to, I want to see an up-to-date list of his financial assets, along with all the more mundane things, like a list of bills he's sponsored, votes he's taken, and public statements he's made. And I want it all reported and available online in a timely fashion."

This vision isn't all that far off. A great deal of this data already exists in digital, downloadable form, though getting more timely and granular reporting remains a struggle. However, even as incumbents resist real-time political disclosure, technology is starting to help with that problem, too. Using everything from mobile phones that can stream video live online to simple text message postings to the micro-blogging service Twitter, millions of people are contributing to a real-time patter of information about what is going on around them. Much of what results is little more than noise and a fair dose of misinformation, but simple filtering tools are making it much easier to find information of value.

As more people play with and pay attention to these tools, the day approaches when citizen watchdogs will start documenting the real-time interactions inside Washington with a startling level of detail. Picture this: a tourist visiting her

Congressman's office happens to overhear a lobbyist rushing in to demand a quick meeting with the representative. Her curiosity piqued, she whips out her smartphone, searches for the name of the lobbyist and discovers he's representing a group her Congressman has supposedly pledged to oppose. So she decides to wait around, and a few minutes later is rewarded by the sight of her representative backslapping the lobbyist as they exit the Congressman's office. She pulls out her phone to take what appears to be a picture, but actually it's a video.

Minutes after it happens, the video of the Congressman and his unlikely lobbyist pal is viewable on the web. Not only that, an archived version of the video is up there too, in a format making it easy to embed on other sites, just like a YouTube video. In addition, all the woman's friends have already gotten an automatic alert, saying "watch me live, now," most likely through Twitter, and a few of them have. Soon, other bloggers are hearing about the video and beginning the important next step of digging into the lobbyist's connections to the Congressman, from campaign contributions to social relationships, and figuring out their significance. It may sound far-fetched, but this kind of real-time, crowdsourced, data-driven transparency is already completely feasible. All the technological and informational pieces exist for it to happen.

As we head into a world where bottom-up, user-generated transparency is becoming more of a reality, the question for our leaders is whether they will embrace this change and show that they have nothing to hide. Will they work harder to align their actions with their words, instead of trying to speak from both sides of their mouths and substitute spin for candor? Instead of giving out as little information as possible, will they actively share all that is relevant to their government service with the people who pay their salaries? Will they trust the public to understand the complexities of that information, instead of treating them like children who can't handle the truth? And will we as citizens show that we do understand, and appreciate being dealt with as full participants, and accept that governing a modern society is complicated? If we want more transparency, we also have to allow our leaders to admit their mistakes. Otherwise, the cycle of denial, and denial of truth, will not end.

7

The End of Secrecy

In one direction we can reach out and touch the time when the leaders of the Soviet Union thought that the explosion at the nuclear reactor in Chernobyl could be kept secret from the rest of the world. In the other direction we can see a time—already upon us—when fourteen-year-old hackers in Australia or Newfoundland can make their way into the most sensitive areas of national security or international finance. The central concern of government in the future will not be information, but analysis. We need government agencies staffed with argumentative people who can live with ambiguity and look upon secrecy as a sign of insecurity.
> —Daniel Patrick Moynihan, Chairman's Foreword,
> Report on the Commission on Protecting and Reducing
> Government Secrets, 1997

Three may keep a secret if two of them are dead.
> —Benjamin Franklin

For some time now, our political leaders have been saying that they understand, nay, that they embrace, the disruptive potential of the Internet. Take President Obama, who used the Internet so adroitly in his 2008 election campaign. Here he is talking about the power of the Internet at a town hall meeting with students in Shanghai in 2009, where he memorably declared:

> I am a big believer in technology and I'm a big believer in openness when it comes to the flow of information. I think that the more freely information flows, the stronger the society becomes, because then citizens of countries around the world can hold their own governments accountable. They can begin to think for themselves. That generates new ideas. It encourages creativity.

Obama added, "The truth is that because in the United States information is free, and I have a lot of critics in the United States who can say all kinds of things about me, I actually think that that makes our democracy stronger and it makes me a better leader because it forces me to hear opinions that I don't want to hear."[1]

Or take British Prime Minister David Cameron, another big believer in how being networked is changing society. Here he is speaking at the TED conference in February 2010, before his election, about what he called "the next age of government":

> Think about how all of you have changed the way we shop, the way we travel, the way that business is done. That has already happened; the information and Internet revolution has actually gone all the way through our societies in so many different ways, but it hasn't in every way yet touched our government. So, how could this happen? Well,

I think there are three chief ways that it should make an enormous difference, in transparency, in greater choice, and in accountability, in giving us that genuine people power.[2]

His counterpart, former Prime Minister Gordon Brown, was equally effusive. Here he is speaking at the TED conference a year earlier, when he was still leading government: "Foreign policy can never be the same again. It cannot be run by elites; it's got to be run by listening to the public opinions of peoples who are blogging, who are communicating with each other around the world."[3]

Theirs has been a kind of bloodless embrace, a rhetorical gesture to a changing culture without any real content and certainly no loss of control. As described in previous chapters, most of what they've done with the Internet has been without cost to them. Yes, it was gratifying to see David Cameron open himself up, when he was the opposition party leader, to voter-generated questions on his Webcameron site, where indeed the wisdom of the crowd forced him to answer some queries he might have preferred to avoid. But since becoming prime minister, he's closed down that channel for occasional dissent. And yes, as a candidate Obama allowed his supporters to use his online social network, my.BarackObama.com, to organize a 20,000-strong petition objecting to his flip-flopping on his position on warrantless wiretapping. But after an email response and a few hours of some of his policy advisers

deflecting questions on his blog, the issue was dropped.[4]
The Internet has been a tool for politicians like Obama to
consolidate their power, not to empower others for any other
purpose.

To be sure, they've been fascinated by the Internet's
potential to challenge the status quo elsewhere. President
Obama deftly used YouTube to address the Iranian
people directly at the beginning of his administration,
posting a message of friendship at the time of the Nowruz
(springtime) celebrations that, according to YouTube's
open tracking analytics, was indeed widely watched inside
Iran.[5] And administration officials have spoken out often
in defense of bloggers' free speech rights, and condemning
countries like China, Egypt, Iran, Tunisia, Uzbekistan, and
Vietnam for clamping down on the Internet and cracking
down on human rights activists using online social network
platforms.

But the reason the current confrontation between
WikiLeaks and the United States government is a pivotal
event is that, unlike these other applications of technology to
politics, this time the free flow of information is threatening
the American establishment with difficult questions. And
not at the level of embarrassing one politician or bureaucrat
but by exposing systemic details of how America actually
conducts its foreign and military policies. Or, as writer Bruce
Sterling memorably put it, "Julian Assange has hacked a

superpower."[6] The result is a series of deeply uncomfortable contradictions.

In the days after the State Department cables starting leaking, not only did Senator Joe Lieberman intimidate major Internet companies into kicking WikiLeaks off their services without any serious review, the government told its own employees that they shouldn't look at references to WikiLeaks from government computers or their home computers, and even public resources like the Library of Congress started filtering searches on its computers and Wi-Fi to prevent people from reading news articles about the cables.[7] The Office of Management and Budget circulated a fourteen-page memo to all government agencies requiring them to tighten their security procedures, which included suggestions that they employ psychiatrists and sociologists to measure employee "despondence and grumpiness as a means to gauge waning trustworthiness," "capture evidence of pre-employment and/ or post-employment activities or participation in on-line media data mining sites like WikiLeaks or Open Leaks," and require all employees to report their contacts with the media.[8] It was quite an about-face from the OMB's Open Government Directive of a year earlier, which called on agencies to "create an unprecedented and sustained level of openness and accountability."[9]

And the Justice Department began pursuing a criminal investigation against WikiLeaks, demanding that Twitter turn over the subscriber account information—including personal addresses, connections made to and from the account, IP addresses used, means of payment (though Twitter is free)—for Julian Assange, Bradley Manning, and three other people who had been involved with the group around the time that the Collateral Murder video came out: Icelandic MP Birgitta Jonsdottir, Dutch hacker Rop Gonggrijp, and American anticensorship hacker Jacob Appelbaum. This is an extremely worrisome development. For there is nothing that WikiLeaks has done that is different from any other newspaper or media outlet that has received leaked government documents, verified their authenticity, and then published their contents and analysis. If WikiLeaks can be prosecuted and convicted for its acts of journalism, then the foundations of freedom of the press in America are in serious trouble.

No one American official has been more eloquent in her expressions of support for the power of the Internet than U.S. Secretary of State Hillary Clinton. Under her leadership, the State Department has expanded its use of social media, developed initiatives to support the use of mobile phones for raising money to aid victims of natural disasters in Pakistan and Haiti, launched a "Virtual Student Foreign Service" program to involve college students in online public diplomacy, and organized several visible technology delegations and training workshops to foster greater use of modern tools to strengthen civil society organizations. (Full disclosure: Personal Democracy Forum, the organization I run with Andrew Rasiej, was hired by the State Department's e-Diplomacy division to produce a one-day "TechCamp" held in Santiago, Chile on November 20, 2010, for about fifty civil society leaders across Latin America, and we also received support from the U.S. Embassy in Spain to help pay for the travel costs of American speakers to our PdF Europe conferences.)

Clinton gave a highly visible speech on "Internet Freedom" on January 21, 2010 in Washington, where she declared:

> The spread of information networks is forming a new nervous system for our planet . . . in many respects, information has never been so free. There are more ways to spread more ideas to more people than at any moment in history. And even in authoritarian countries, information networks are helping people discover new facts and making governments more accountable. . . . The Internet is a network that magnifies the power and potential of all others. And that's why we believe it's critical that its users are assured certain basic freedoms. Freedom of expression is first among them. This freedom is no longer defined solely by whether citizens can go into the town square and criticize their government without fear of retribution. Blogs, emails, social networks, and text messages have opened up new forums for exchanging ideas, and created new targets for censorship.
>
> Some countries have erected electronic barriers that prevent their people from accessing portions of the world's networks. They've expunged words, names, and phrases from search engine

results. They have violated the privacy of citizens who engage in non-violent political speech.

Realigning our policies and our priorities will not be easy. But adjusting to new technology rarely is. When the telegraph was introduced, it was a source of great anxiety for many in the diplomatic community, where the prospect of receiving daily instructions from capitals was not entirely welcome. But just as our diplomats eventually mastered the telegraph, they are doing the same to harness the potential of these new tools as well.

Now, ultimately, this issue isn't just about information freedom; it is about what kind of world we want and what kind of world we will inhabit. It's about whether we live on a planet with one Internet, one global community, and a common body of knowledge that benefits and unites us all, or a fragmented planet in which access to information and opportunity is dependent on where you live and the whims of censors.

The idea that this wondrous "new nervous system" for the planet might want to turn its attention on the most powerful country on the planet shouldn't be a shock to leaders like Clinton, but when the State Department cables started to leak, she fell back on a much older way of seeing the world. "The United States strongly condemns the illegal disclosure of classified information," she said in her prepared statement the day the news broke. "It puts people's lives in danger, threatens our national security, and undermines our efforts to work with other countries to solve shared problems." She added later, "Disclosures like these tear at the fabric of the proper function of responsible government." The notion that lying to the

American public, or the world, about the conduct of foreign or military policy might be more damaging to the fabric of international relations or to the functioning of responsible government, was not addressed.

On the morning of July 7, 2005, ten minutes before nine, suicide bombers blew themselves on three trains on the London Underground. Less than an hour later, a bus was blown up as well. Fifty-five people were killed. For the first three hours of the crisis, the government said the incidents were actually due to some kind of power surge in the electric grid serving the trains. But within the first hour and twenty minutes, there were 1,300 blog posts indicating that these were bombings. The BBC News alone received 20,000 emails, 3,000 text messages, a thousand digital pictures, and twenty video clips, confirming the essence of this terrible news.

On May 8, 2009, the British newspaper *The Telegraph* began publishing the unexpurgated expense records of members of the British Parliament, which were leaked to it by John Wick, a former SAS officer who was the intermediary for an anonymous source. That person's name has never been revealed, but it is believed to be someone who had been involved in a secret effort by House of Commons staff to censor the records prior to them being released in response to years of Freedom of Information requests from journalist Heather Brooke. As she writes in her book *Silent State*, "Some of the staff were so disgusted by what they saw and by the lies being told about the delays that they made a copy of the data. A mole inside the 'redaction room' made a copy and later passed it to John Wick."[10]

Wick says that he was also told that critical information was being removed from the files that would prevent many of the expense scandals from ever being revealed. And, says, Wick, "The ultimate source was adamant that the key thing was that both the information and the way in which it was handled should be in the public domain and that its release was in the public interest." Wick himself told the press he was personally dismayed at how much information the government was collecting on the public, and how poorly it managed to keep that information private. "We've reached the stage in society where they want to know everything about us, I think we're entitled to know about them."[11]

I offer these two seemingly disparate anecdotes to make a point about what they have in common. In the first case, real news was reported by ordinary people faster than the authorities could construct an official narrative. The government's failure to tell a truth that the public already knew damaged its authority. In the second case, real news was released by ordinary people, in the face of the desire of the authorities to maintain an official but false narrative. The government's failure to tell the truth that the public found out despite its efforts damaged its authority. In both cases, free agents are the sources of truths more credible than anything the government offers. And in both cases, it is the same human impulse to share the truth that shines through. Now, think about Bradley Manning and what motivated him.

In the networked age, where the watched can also be the watchers, what is at stake is nothing less than the credibility of authority itself. Western governments presumably rest on the consent of the governed, but only if the governed trust the word of those who would govern them. In this changed environment, the people formerly known as the authorities can re-earn that trust only by being more transparent, and by eliminating the contradictions between what they say and what they actually do. Compounding this challenge, today when a crisis strikes, information moves faster than the "authorities" can know using their own, slower methods. WikiLeaks, and other channels for the unauthorized release and spread of information, are symptoms of this change, not its cause.

Two years ago, all of this was laid out brilliantly by Nik Gowing, the main presenter for the BBC World News, in a long paper he wrote for the Reuters Institute for the Study of Journalism called "'Skyful of Lies' and Black Swans: The new tyranny of shifting information power in crises." (I paraphrased the story above of the London subway and bus bombings from his essay.) Gowing writes about a world where "information doers"—people with access to real-time information and the ability to share it—can unmake the credibility of authorities with little more than a click of a mouse: "They shed light where it is often assumed officially there will be darkness." He argues:

> In a crisis there is a relentless and unforgiving trend towards an ever greater information transparency. In the most remote and hostile locations of the globe, hundreds of millions of electronic eyes and ears are creating a capacity for scrutiny and new demands for accountability. It is way beyond the assumed power and influence of the traditional media. This global electronic reach catches institutions unaware and surprises with what it reveals.
>
> Overall, this surge of civilian information is having an asymmetric, negative impact on the traditional structures of power. It is subverting their effectiveness, and calling into question institutional assumptions that as organs of power they will function efficiently and with public confidence. With few exceptions, institutions of state, political and corporate power remain largely in denial about the inexorable negative impact on their reputations and the public's perceptions. Yet it is in times of acute crisis that expectations for effective action are greatest and most pressing.

Gowing spent months talking to current and former government ministers, civil servants, corporate executives, academics, and media professionals as he developed his report. And what he discovered was depressing and worrisome. For all the supposed awareness of the new media system, few had budged at all in their approach to information sharing. "In government cabinet rooms, ministerial offices, military and security command HQs, or many corporate board rooms there is little fundamental systemic change either to embrace or to match the hyper rates of technological media developments," Gowing reports. "This is even though most of those involved readily use privately the cheap, lightweight technology that now challenges their professional duties," he adds, drily.

Few seemed willing to confront the likelihood that a "Black Swan" event could occur to them, preferring to believe that such creatures don't even exist. (The "skyful of lies" is what the Burmese junta called all the digital media that prodemocracy protestors shared with each other and the world during the September 2007 protests there.) Gowing discovered that, again and again, the so-called authorities preferred to hide the truth rather than admit error. In particular, his paper documents many troubling examples of lying by police and military officials that have been exposed by the unexpected but predictable presence of "information doers" on the scene. They range from a video that a New York investment banker happened to take when newsstand salesman Ian Tomlinson was hit by a policeman's baton during protests against the G-20 meeting in London, causing his death (the police claimed he died of a heart attack but a later investigation found otherwise), to a mobile phone video of dozens of victims of a U.S. Air Force missile strike on an Afghani school (the military claimed only seven people were killed; a subsequent investigation found at least fifty-five people died).

But, writes Gowing, "The 'courtiers [in government

systems] like behavior that masks the truth' was how one former senior government figure described institutional reactions to the new reality. They tend to 'ratchet up old means of control' rather than embracing new liberating principles."[12]

In the case of WikiLeaks and Cablegate, these painful contradictions could have been averted had the State Department responded positively to Julian Assange's offer in November to help redact information that the government felt needed to be kept out of public view. "Subject to the general objective of ensuring maximum disclosure of information in the public interest, WikiLeaks would be grateful for the United States government to privately nominate any specific instances (record numbers or names) where it considers the publication of information would put individual persons at significant risk of harm that has not already been addressed," Assange wrote the U.S. ambassador in London. He also promised to keep any such consultation confidential. In response, Harold Koh, the State Department legal advisor, wrote back to Assange rejecting his offer, demanding the return of the leaked material, and insisting that any publication of the cables would "place at risk the lives of countless innocent individuals."[13] (This statement, however, did not prevent the State Department and other government agencies from giving *The New York Times* detailed advice on what material to redact when that paper's reporters sought counsel.)[14]

WikiLeaks, and other entities inspired by it that are beginning to spread, presents the United States with an especially difficult version of the information doer problem, because the discovery of new facts may now occur at any time. Unfortunately there is a large gap between what American officials have told the public about their actions, and what they have actually done. Transparency may be the best medicine for a healthy democracy, but the problem with the WikiLeaks revelations from the Iraq and Afghanistan wars, plus the State Department cables, may well be that they expose too much. Not in the sense of giving away military secrets that endanger troops in the field or human rights workers; so far both the Pentagon and the State Department have explicitly admitted that no such harm has occurred (though the original release of the Afghan war records may have placed some civilian informants in danger from the Taliban).[15]

Rather, the war logs and diplomatic cables show that the nine-year war in Afghanistan is doomed. And this is not something the governments fighting that war want to tell their publics. As Javier Moreno, the editor of *El País*, wrote in a long essay explaining why his paper decided to work with WikiLeaks on publishing the State Department cables,

> Tens of thousands of soldiers are fighting a war in Afghanistan that their respective leaders know is not winnable. Tens of thousands of soldiers are shoring up a government known around the world

to be corrupt, but which is tolerated by those who sent the soldiers there in the first place. The WikiLeaks cables show that none of the Western powers believes that Afghanistan can become a credible nation in the medium term, and much less become a viable democracy, despite the stated aims of those whose soldiers are fighting and dying there. Few people have been surprised to learn that the Afghan president has been salting away millions of dollars in overseas aid in foreign bank accounts with the full cognizance of his patrons.

Meanwhile, next door, Pakistan is awash with corruption as well. It also has a decaying nuclear arsenal that is a major security risk. The country funds terrorist activity against its neighbor India and many countries in the West. Money from Saudi Arabia and the Gulf emirates is also used to fund Sunni terrorist groups; but as these governments are allies of the United States, Washington prefers to remain silent, excluding them from its list of sponsors of terrorism or those belonging to what the Bush regime dubbed "the axis of evil." Clinton, or one of her direct subordinates, gave the order to carry out espionage within the United Nations, and not just on representatives of so-called rogue states, but on the UN secretary general himself. In turn, he has so far failed to demand an explication for this flagrant breach of international law.

We may have suspected our governments of underhand dealings, but we did not have the proof that WikiLeaks has provided. We now know that our governments were aware of the situations mentioned above, and, what is more, they have hidden the facts from us.[16]

Instead of an honest discussion about what the war logs and cables tell us in toto, in the wake of their emergence we have been treated to a bizarre and contradictory set of responses. Sometimes, what WikiLeaks has done is portrayed as worse than what Al Qaeda has done. And other times, we are told that the so-called revelations are actually pretty humdrum. Nothing to see here; move along please.

On the one hand, there are the angry calls for Assange's prosecution, persecution or simple assassination from the likes of former House Speaker Newt Gingrich ("He should be treated as an enemy combatant and WikiLeaks should be closed down permanently and decisively");[17] former Alaska governor Sarah Palin ("Why was he not pursued with the same urgency that we pursue al Qaeda and Taliban leaders?");[18] former Senator Rick Santorum ("What he's doing is terrorism, in my opinion");[19] *Weekly Standard* editor Bill Kristol ("Why can't we use our various assets to harass, snatch or neutralize Julian Assange and his collaborators, wherever they are?");[20] and Democratic political consultant Bob Beckel ("This guy's a traitor. . . . And I'm not for the death penalty. So . . . there's only one way to do it: illegally shoot the son of a bitch.").[21] Perhaps most dangerous demands like those of Republican Representative Peter King, a senior member of the House Committee on Homeland Security, to have WikiLeaks declared a "foreign terrorist organization." That would have the effect of giving the United States government the power not only to seize WikiLeaks' funds but also, as King put it, to "go after anyone who provides them with any help or contributions or assistance whatsoever."[22]

But other authorities have been much calmer in their

response. Most notably, Defense Secretary Robert Gates (reportedly a close ally of Hillary Clinton), said on November 30, 2010:

> Now, I've heard the impact of these releases on our foreign policy described as a meltdown, as a game-changer, and so on. I think those descriptions are fairly significantly overwrought. The fact is, governments deal with the United States because it's in their interest, not because they like us, not because they trust us, and not because they believe we can keep secrets. Many governments—some governments—deal with us because they fear us, some because they respect us, most because they need us. We are still essentially, as has been said before, the indispensable nation. So other nations will continue to deal with us. They will continue to work with us. We will continue to share sensitive information with one another. Is this embarrassing? Yes. Is it awkward? Yes. Consequences for U.S. foreign policy? I think fairly modest.[23]

And writing in *Time* magazine, Fareed Zakaria, one of the country's leading foreign policy pundits, insisted that "the sum total of the output I have read is actually quite reassuring about the way Washington—or at least the State Department—works."[24] Secretary of State Clinton took a similar approach a few days after the cables started to emerge, noting, "What you see are diplomats doing the work of diplomacy: reporting and analyzing and providing information, solving problems, worrying about big, complex challenges."[25]

Vice President Joe Biden actually stated both positions in one twenty-four-hour period, as noted by blogger Glenn Greenwald, who has been vociferous in his defense of

WikiLeaks. On December 16, Biden told MSNBC's Andrew Mitchell that the leaks were no big deal: "I don't think there's any substantive damage, no. Look, some of the cables are embarrassing . . . but nothing that I'm aware of that goes to the essence of the relationship that would allow another nation to say: 'they lied to me, we don't trust them.'" A day later, he told David Gregory of *Meet the Press*, "This guy has done things that have damaged and put in jeopardy the lives and occupations of other parts of the world. He's made it more difficult for us to conduct our business with our allies and our friends."[26]

There are also signs that the government is deliberately overstating the seriousness of the leaks in order to intimidate Internet service providers and push WikiLeaks off the Internet without a criminal conviction. Reuters's Mark Hosenball reported in mid-January 2011 that State Department officials were privately telling Congress that the revelations were "embarrassing but not damaging."[27] This after a speech by State Department spokesman P. J. Crowley where he insisted, "From our standpoint, there has been serious damage."[28]

Amazingly, all of these commentators have been announcing their judgments about the cables' importance, or lack thereof, while barely one percent of the actual leaked trove has been published. But maybe they can't be blamed for thinking that the first weeks' stories on the now-public material was indeed the whole cache, given how poorly the media has covered this basic fact. Again and again, Assange has been accused of indiscriminately publishing the entire archive of cables that Bradley Manning leaked to him, when by early February 2011 only about 3,900 cables had been released, and nearly all of those through a process of collaboration, redaction, and editing with WikiLeaks' major newspaper partners. For example, Senator Dianne Feinstein started a *Wall Street Journal* op-ed calling for Assange's prosecution under the Espionage Act with these words, "When WikiLeaks founder Julian Assange released his latest document trove— more than 250,000 secret State Department cables—he intentionally harmed the U.S. government."[29] Dozens of news organizations made the same error, with only a few posting later corrections.[30]

There is only one way to reconcile these seemingly contradictory messages coming from the U.S. government and its allies in Congress and the media. At some fundamental level, they probably understand that the conditions for maintaining their monopoly on critical information have been broken. But they apparently still hope that the next Bradley Manning might be dissuaded from an act of conscience if he believes that either the personal cost will be too high, or that his actions won't make a difference. Of course, neither approach will work, as long as millions of other government employees can also access the information that the government is trying to hide.

Let's posit that what Julian Assange is doing is "radical transparency," that is, publishing everything he can get his hands on. He has not, in fact, been doing that, though he is obviously publishing a great deal of raw material. Given that the Internet is a realm of abundance—not scarcity like the old ink-based and airtime-based media—this is a feature, not a bug. Raw data dumps of previously private or secret information are now part of the media landscape. As Max Frankel, former executive editor of *The New York Times*, recently put it, "The threat of massive leaks will persist so long as there are massive secrets."[31]

Security expert Bruce Schneier makes a similar point. "Secrets are only as secure as the least trusted person who knows them," he wrote on his blog a few weeks after Cablegate started. "The more people who know a secret, the more likely it is to be made public." Somewhere between 500,000 and 600,000 military and diplomatic personnel had access to the SIPRNet system that Manning tapped. The government actually doesn't know precisely how many people overall have security clearances to access classified information.[32] Based on reporting from the Government Accountability Office, Steven Aftergood, a secrecy expert, estimates the number is 2.5 million people.[33] "The top-secret world the government created in response to the terrorist attacks of September 11, 2001, has become so large, so unwieldy and so secretive that no one knows how much money it costs, how many people it employs, how many programs exist within it or exactly how many agencies do the same work," *The Washington Post* recently reported.[34] Schneier adds:

> This has little to do with WikiLeaks. WikiLeaks is just a website. The real story is that "least trusted person" who decided to violate his security clearance and make these cables public. In the 1970s, he would have mailed them to a newspaper. Today, he used WikiLeaks. Tomorrow, he will have his choice of a dozen similar websites. If WikiLeaks didn't exist, he could have made them available via BitTorrent [a distributed file-sharing tool].

In other words, given that this kind of "radical transparency" is technologically feasible, like it or not, it is now a given of our times. Efforts to stop it will fail, just as efforts to stop file-sharing by killing Napster failed. As Schneier sagely points out, "And just as the music and movie industries are going to have to change their business models for the Internet era, governments are going to have to change their secrecy models. I don't know what those new models will be, but they will be different."[35]

Fourteen years ago, Senator Daniel Patrick Moynihan led a bipartisan Commission on Protecting and Reducing Government Secrecy. Its recommendations are worth revisiting in light of WikiLeaks. "It is time for a new way of thinking about secrecy," the commission's report began. "Secrecy is a form of government regulation. Americans are familiar with the tendency to over-regulate in other areas. What is different with secrecy is that the public cannot know the extent or the content of the regulation." The Moynihan Commission was examining a condition not unlike the present day, where millions of people had security clearances and hundreds of thousands of new "top secret" documents, whose disclosure could presumably cause "exceptionally grave damage to the national security," were created each year. But the commission was convinced that the culture of secrecy in government was out of control and hurting the country:

> Excessive secrecy has significant consequences for the national interest when, as a result, policymakers are not fully informed, government is not held accountable for its actions, and the public cannot engage in informed debate. This remains a dangerous world; some secrecy is vital to save lives, bring miscreants to justice, protect national security, and engage in effective diplomacy. Yet as Justice Potter Stewart noted in his opinion in the Pentagon Papers case, when everything is secret, nothing is secret. Even as billions of dollars are spent each year on government secrecy, the classification and personnel security systems have not always succeeded at their core task of protecting those secrets most critical to the national security. The classification system, for example, is used too often to deny the public an understanding of the policymaking process, rather than for the necessary protection of intelligence activities and other highly sensitive matters.[36]

In his own foreword to the report, Moynihan added his own wry observations on how overclassification can make government dumber. "In a culture of secrecy, that which is not secret is easily disregarded or dismissed," he wrote. "Secrecy can be a source of dangerous ignorance."

Daniel Ellsberg makes a very similar point in his autobiography *Secrets: A Memoir of Vietnam and the Pentagon Papers*. Ellsberg was a defense analyst with top security clearances for many years before he decided to leak the Pentagon Papers. He had worked on nuclear war planning policy for the National Security Council before studying Vietnam policy for the Pentagon and State Department. In the fall of 1968, he was working for the Rand Corporation, still with his clearances, and was part of a group tasked by Henry Kissinger—the incoming national security adviser to President-elect Richard Nixon—to prepare a study of options for the new president on Vietnam. While presenting that report to Kissinger, he tried to warn of the dangers of relying too much on top secret information. Here's how he recounts that moment in his book:

> Kissinger was not rushing to end our conversation that morning, and I had one more message to give him. "Henry, there's something I would like to tell you, for what it's worth, something I wish I had been told years ago. You've been a consultant for a long time, and you've dealt a great deal with top secret information. But you're about to receive a whole slew of special clearances, maybe fifteen or twenty of them, that are higher than top secret.
>
> "I've had a number of these myself, and I've known other people who have just acquired them, and I have a pretty good sense of what the effects of receiving these clearances are on a person who didn't

previously know that they even *existed*. And the effect of reading the information that they will make available to you.

"First, you'll be exhilarated by some of this new information, and by having it all—so much! incredible!—suddenly available to you. But second, almost as fast, you will feel like a fool for having studied, written, talked about these subjects, criticized and analyzed decisions made by presidents for years without having known of the existence of all this information, which presidents and others had and you didn't, and which must have influenced their decisions in ways you couldn't even guess. In particular, you'll feel foolish for having literally rubbed shoulders for over a decade with some officials and consultants who did have access to all this information you didn't know about and didn't know they had, and you'll be stunned that they kept that secret from you so well.

"You will feel like a fool, and that will last for about two weeks. Then, after you've started reading all this daily intelligence input and become used to using what amounts to whole libraries of hidden information, which is much more closely held than mere top secret data, you will forget there ever was a time when you didn't have it, and you'll be aware only of the fact that you have it now and most others don't . . . and that all those other people are fools.

"Over a longer period of time—not too long, but a matter of two or three years—you'll eventually become aware of the limitations of this information. There is a great deal that it doesn't tell you, it's often inaccurate, and it can lead you astray just as much as the New York *Times* can. But that takes a while to learn.

"In the meantime, it will have become very hard for you to learn from anybody who doesn't have these clearances. Because you'll be thinking as you listen to them: 'What would this man be telling me if he knew what I know? Would he be giving me the same advice, or would it totally change his predictions and recommendations?' And that mental exercise is so torturous that after a while you give it up and just stop listening. I've seen this with my superiors, my colleagues . . . and with myself.

"You will deal with a person who doesn't have those clearances only from the point of view of what you want him to believe and what impression you want him to go away with, since you'll have to lie carefully to him about what you know. In effect, you will have to manipulate him. You'll give up trying to assess what he has to say. The danger is, you'll become something like a moron. You'll become incapable of learning from most people in the world, no matter how much experience they may have in their particular areas that may be much greater than yours."[37]

Back in 1997, Senator Moynihan already foresaw that the information age would make the culture of government secrecy untenable, even picturing a time "when fourteen-year-old hackers in Australia or Newfoundland" could penetrate the government's most sensitive secrets. He tried, with his commission, which was actually mandated by an act of Congress, to turn the paradigm on its head. "The great discovery of Western science, somewhere in the seventeenth century," he wrote, "was the principle of openness. A scientist who judged he had discovered something, published it. Often to great controversy, leading to rejection, acceptance, modification, whatever. Which is to say, to knowledge. In this setting science advanced, as nowhere else and never before."[38]

It is long past time for government to embrace this paradigm. "Where you're open, things will not be

WikiLeaked," says Christopher Graham, the U.K.'s Information Minister. "Quite a lot of this is only exciting because we didn't know it." He adds, "The best form of defense is transparency—much more proactive publication of what organizations do. It's an attitude of 'OK. You want to know? Here it is.'"[39] Jeff Jarvis, a professor at the CUNY Journalism School in New York, argues that government should be transparent by default, and have to justify when it chooses to make something secret, not the reverse. And he too sees something positive in the impact of WikiLeaks. "Perhaps the lesson of WikiLeaks should be that the open air is less fearsome than we'd thought," he blogged. "That should lead to less secrecy. After all, the only sure defense against leaks is transparency."[40]

People who think that more transparency will only lead to the hiding of secrets deeper in the bureaucracy, or that it will prevent government officials from conducting any kind of meaningful business, and that as a result we will know less, not more, about the workings of government or the powerful should think again. By that logic, we should require less public disclosure of what the government does, not more. Why ask campaign contributors or lobbyists to disclose any of their activities? In fact, when people think what they're doing might be subject to public view, their behavior generally changes for the better. Thus the overall value of Cablegate—exposing a great deal of the world's sovereign powers to a new level of public scrutiny, and warning them that more such scrutiny is always a possibility in the future—should, on balance, lead to better behavior. Why? Because the cost of maintaining the contradictions between what you say in public and what you do in reality has just gone up another notch.

Carne Ross is a British diplomat who resigned his post at the United Nations over the dissimulation that his government practiced during the lead-up to the invasion of Iraq in 2003. "From now on, it will be ever more difficult for governments to claim one thing and do another," says Ross. "For in making such claims, they are making themselves vulnerable to WikiLeaks of their own."[41] If all it takes is one person with a USB drive, the "least trusted person" who may feel some contradiction in his or her government's behavior prick his conscience, that information can move into public view more easily than ever before. That is today's new reality of the twenty-first century. It would be far better for all of us if our governments and other powerful institutions got with the business of accepting that transparency will be a new fact of life, and take real steps to align their words with their deeds. In that respect, Hillary Clinton should thank Julian Assange, rather than apologize to world leaders for what he did.

It should go without saying that transparency does not mean exposing *everyone's* secrets to public view. But given how much our privacy is already being eroded, not just by government but also by private corporations, it's an understandable concern. It is striking to see how often people react to the news about WikiLeaks by asking how they could possibly do their jobs if every confidential conversation or negotiation were required to be public. But the transparency movement isn't aimed at exposing the doings of ordinary people to intense scrutiny, and the kind of network effects that occur around instances of information censorship generally don't happen around spreading someone's shopping list.

As Julian Assange argued as recently as the middle of January 2011, "Transparency should be proportional to the power that one has. The more power one has, the greater the dangers generated by that power, and the more need for transparency. Conversely, the weaker one is, the more danger there is in being transparent."[42] In other words, if information is power, then what the transparency movement is trying to do is correct an asymmetric power relationship.

This can be a messy process, and both the holders and the sharers of previously secret or hidden information need to act with care. I have a vivid memory of being accosted at some organization's annual dinner by the chief of staff of a liberal member of Congress furious that her personal financial disclosure statement, which not only listed her salary but her bank and IRA account records and home address, had been put online at a site called Legistorm by a journalist-entrepreneur named Jock Friedly.[43] Even though these disclosures had always been "public" in the sense of being available for viewing in a basement office in the Capitol, this felt different to her. In addition, a number of staffers had inadvertently disclosed more personal details than required by law, and were now worried about the risks of identity theft. Around the same time, the Sunlight Foundation's researchers discovered that the government was inadvertently disclosing the Social Security numbers of some grant recipients in the course of placing federal spending information online. Redaction of private details that have no reason to be in public view is a vital part of responsible transparency efforts.

But it is critical to recognize that transparency is a necessary corrective to excessive government power. What we are pressing for is not the power to be Big Brother, watching everyone from above, but rather a flock of Little Sisters, watching government from below. All that the WikiLeaks phenomenon adds to that effort is the ability to share information beyond the control of any one government's laws limiting that effort. Speaking at a January 24, 2011, PdF symposium on WikiLeaks and Internet freedom, Clay Shirky made yet another of his always-fresh observations. After World War II, he told the audience, the United States, United Kingdom, Canada, Australia, and New Zealand formed a secret pact building on their cooperation during the war in sharing intelligence gathered from eavesdropping. Since each country's intelligence service was forbidden by local law to spy on its own citizens, but nothing prevented each service from spying on other countries, the five members of what is known as UKUSA agreed to share information on each other's citizens, essentially going around their own local laws. To Shirky, what WikiLeaks represents is the parallel formation of a civic intelligence network, one that has also found a way to route around the laws of any one state. "WikiLeaks does not have to play an iterated game of Prisoner's Dilemma with the U.S.," Shirky wrote in a recent blog post on this same theme. "Not only is WikiLeaks not housed in the U.S., it isn't housed in any single other nation the U.S. could complain to. They can defect at will."[44]

And like it or not, this is fundamentally disruptive to the old balance of power politics. Dispersed networks and powerful encryption technologies are taking away some of the long-held advantages that state actors have had over their subjects. As Internet freedom activist (and science fiction novelist) Cory Doctorow wrote recently, "Poorly resourced individuals and groups with cheap, old computers are able to encipher their messages to an extent that they cannot be deciphered by all the secret police in the world, even if they employ every computer ever built in a gigantic, decades-long project to force the locks off the intercepted message. In this sense, at least, the technological deck is stacked in favour of dissidents—who have never before enjoyed the power to hide their communiqués beyond the reach of secret police—over the state, who have always enjoyed the power to keep secrets from the people."[45]

The bottom line: if you are a private citizen and you want to stay that way, start by not sharing so much of yourself online. Read the "terms of service" that come with all the free online services that everyone is using, and decide if you are comfortable with the possibility that your information may be sold to advertisers, or given to a policeman with a warrant but without your knowledge, or that the privacy settings that you are relying on may be changed without notice. But also understand that the more you do in the public arena, including such basic civic acts as signing a ballot petition or making a campaign donation or getting a government contract, the more information will be asked of and shared about you. And if you are one of the few to whom much power has been given, much more transparency is to be expected.

8

WikiLeaks and the Future of the Transparency Movement

All I want is the truth; just give me some truth.

—*John Lennon*

I may not agree with what you have to say, but I will fight to death for your right to say it.

—*Voltaire*

Julian Assange is not an easy person to work with. When he arrived at the Personal Democracy Forum conference hotel in Barcelona, back in November 2009, the first thing he did upon meeting my colleague Andrew Rasiej was grill him about who our sponsors were and if we had any association with the U.S. Government. (As noted above, the U.S. Embassy in Spain was covering the travel costs of our American speakers, using funds dedicated to supporting cultural and educational exchange.) It took two long conversations with us before he decided that Andrew and I were benevolent, or at least benign, actors and not tools of the government.

Several of Assange's associates have had far more difficult dealings with him. Last summer, after allegations of possible rape or sexual misconduct by Assange started to surface in Sweden, Birgitta Jonsdottir, a member of the Icelandic Parliament who had worked closely with Assange on the Collateral Murder video, spoke out. "I am not angry with Julian, but this is a situation that has clearly gotten out of hand," she told reporter Philip Shenon. "These personal matters should have nothing to do with WikiLeaks. I have strongly urged him to focus on the legalities that he's dealing with and let some other people carry the torch."[1]

She was also growing concerned that WikiLeaks as directed by Assange lacked a clear and accountable structure. Its finances, for example, are not disclosed. Jonsdottir added that, after the wave of international attention prompted by the helicopter video:

> I realized this was going to grow into a massive organization or would bring attention to the organization. I felt it didn't have the structures in place in how to utilize volunteers and security. I was concerned about lack of transparency in relation to the money issues. I wanted a meeting. I became obsessed that we had to have a meeting to create the structures and if you don't have proper structures and a means for people to communicate in a functional way, it's a disaster. I couldn't get the meeting. All the volunteers wanted the meeting except one. He didn't feel it was necessary.[2]

Instead, Jonsdottir left the organization and focused her energies on the Icelandic Modern Media Initiative, an effort that WikiLeaks helped inspire to make Iceland into a safe haven for the most robust investigative journalism possible worldwide.

Jonsdottir wasn't the only person raising concerns about Assange's autocratic management of WikiLeaks or his personal life. Her public comments appeared a few days after *Newsweek* had reported on dissension within the group. According to reporter Mark Hosenball, many WikiLeaks activists in Europe "were privately concerned that Assange has continued to spread allegations of dirty tricks and hint at conspiracies against him without justification. Insiders say that some people affiliated with the website are already brainstorming whether there might be some way to persuade their front man to step aside, or failing that, even to oust him."[3]

This story led to a confrontation between Assange and Daniel Domscheit-Berg, who was until then the second-most visible representative of WikiLeaks. According to a chat log between them obtained by Wired.com, Domscheit-Berg started by challenging Assange's unilateral decision to arrange for the release of the Iraq War logs in concert with several major media organizations on a timetable that some volunteers thought too hasty. But even before answering Domscheit-Berg's question, Assange accused him of being the source of the *Newsweek* story. While he denied that was the case, Domscheit-Berg insisted, "You should face this, rather than trying to shoot at the only person that even cares to be honest about it towards you." Referring to members of Germany's famed Chaos Computer Club, who had been supporting WikiLeaks to a large degree, Domscheit-Berg added, "This debate is fuckin all over the place, and no one understands why you go into denial, especially not the people that know about other incidents."

Assange declared that he was investigating "a serious security breach." Domscheit-Berg fired back, "I am investigating a serious breach in trust." After Assange threatened to fire Domscheit-Berg, he responded, "You are not anyone's king or god. And you're not even fulfilling your role as a leader right now. A leader communicates and cultivates trust in himself. You are doing the exact opposite. You behave like some kind of emperor or slave trader." Assange suspended Domscheit-Berg for one month, which then led him to quit the group entirely.

A second WikiLeaks volunteer, Herbert Snorrason, who had helped oversee WikiLeaks' secure chat room, then questioned Assange's decision to suspend Domscheit-Berg and was slapped back. "I am the heart and soul of this organization, its founder, philosopher, spokesperson, original coder, organizer, financier and all the rest," Assange wrote Snorrason. "If you have a problem with me, piss off."[4]

Assange's autocratic control and his personal problems are not the only problems many people, myself included, have with WikiLeaks itself as a model of twenty-first century transparency activism. First, we need to be clear about which version of the project we are evaluating. Is it the first model, which was essentially a wiki-fied conduit for raw information dumps? That was the case from 2006 through 2009, when for example WikiLeaks posted troves of documents on corruption in Kenya—but it also posted secret sorority hazing rituals, Mormon and Mason rites, even the pirated text of a book on corruption in Kenya, without permission of its author.[5] Or is it the second model, of tight editorial control and production, which is what went into the making and promotion of the Collateral Murder video and website? If so, who is making the editing decisions, and why should whistle-blowers trust that their information will be used appropriately and fairly?

Or is it the third model, which the site has adopted over the last year, where deals are negotiated with major media on the timing of data releases. WikiLeaks now works in cooperation with major news organizations like *The Guardian*, *Der Spiegel*, and *El País*, analyzing, redacting, and releasing documents in a slow and careful process. Even that third model appears to have serious problems. It still vests too much power in Assange personally, as Domscheit-Berg and Snorrason experienced last summer. And it is prone to conflict with those media partners, as Sarah Ellison detailed recently in *Vanity Fair*. According to her report, relations between Assange and *The Guardian* took a bad turn after he suddenly brought the Channel 4 television network in on the release of the Afghan war logs without consulting anyone else. Then, when *The Guardian* managed to obtain a complete set of the State Department cables from a former WikiLeaks volunteer, and began planning to publish its own stories on its own timetable, Assange reportedly threatened to sue the paper, arguing, Ellison writes, "that he owned the information and had a financial interest in how and when it was released."[6] (The conflict was ultimately resolved amicably over much coffee followed by much wine, Ellison reports. More recent accounts by participants in the meetings from *The Guardian* and *Der Spiegel* confirm the gist of her account.)[7]

Another problem with WikiLeaks as a model of transparency activism is that it is not clear what Assange's ultimate goals are, or whether his methods are the best way to achieve them. At first, the site said that its "primary interest is in exposing oppressive regimes in Asia, the former Soviet bloc, Sub-Saharan Africa and the Middle East, but we also expect to be of assistance to people of all regions who wish to reveal unethical behaviour in their governments and corporations."[8] Now it describes itself "as a non-profit media organization dedicated to bringing important news and information to the public. We provide an innovative, secure and anonymous way for independent sources around the world to leak information to our journalists." But it's far from clear that Assange is just interested in exposing oppressive and unethical behavior.

As he was working on the launch of WikiLeaks in November and December 2006, Assange wrote two essays. In them, he talked about wanting to "radically shift regime behavior" and to "change or remove" governments or corporations that he viewed as authoritarian conspiracies. In his analysis, those institutions thrive on their ability to control access to information; mass leaking causes them to become more paranoid, brittle, and incapable of functioning. To Assange, the goal of transparency is not to enable better behavior by government or corporations, but to make it impossible for "the conspiracy to think, act and adapt."[9] There is good reason to believe that this is indeed Assange's aim. Last November, as Cablegate began to break open, blogger Aaron Bady wrote a long essay called "Julian Assange and the Computer Conspiracy; 'To destroy this invisible government,'" pointing to these essays and offering exactly that analysis of Assange's philosophy. WikiLeaks' Twitter account then tweeted a link to Bady's post, reading, "Good essay on one of the key ideas behind WikiLeaks."[10]

If anything, Assange's greatest contribution to global enlightenment is that the idea of a viable "stateless news organization," to use Jay Rosen's phrase, beholden to no country's laws and dedicated to bringing government information into public view, has been set loose into the world. Even if Assange goes to jail and WikiLeaks is somehow shut down, others are already following in his footsteps. Or, as futurist Mark Pesce nicely put it, "The failures of WikiLeaks provide the blueprint for the systems which will follow it."[11] Since Cablegate, several independent WikiLeaks-style projects have announced themselves, including: BrusselsLeaks.com (focused on the European Union); BalkanLeaks.eu (focused on the Balkan countries); Indoleaks.org (focused on Indonesia); Rospil.info (focused on Russia); two competing environmental efforts each claiming the name GreenLeaks; and the Al-Jazeera Transparency Unit, which in late January 2011 began publishing (in tandem with *The Guardian*) a cache of documents from inside the Palestinian Authority that exposed much of the secret Palestinian negotiating strategy with Israel.[12] Some recent graduates of the CUNY Journalism School launched a simple tool for publishers interested in attracting whistleblowers called Localeaks.[13] And even *The New York Times* announced that it was exploring creating a special portal for would-be leakers. Perhaps the most important of these fledgling efforts is OpenLeaks.org, which is being built by Domscheit-Berg, Snorrason and other former WikiLeaks associates. Of all these efforts, OpenLeaks is most likely to have the technological and cryptographic skills needed to succeed in a world filled with shady actors opposed to transparency. And unlike WikiLeaks, it is designed to be decentralized.

In mid-December, Domscheit-Berg told me that OpenLeaks was trying to correct mistakes in WikiLeaks' approach. "I am not into being a leader, and I don't trust the

whole concept of leaders either." He added, "If you follow
the debate around why we left the WL [WikiLeaks] project,
you will find that a strikingly important detail." He described
OpenLeaks as being more of a technological service provider
to lots of media organizations, as well as others with an
interest in opening up information, like nongovernmental
organizations and labor unions. Instead of being a central
hub for leaks, it will provide a dedicated website for handling
leaks to each entity. In his view, this approach has several
advantages:

> Firstly, the system will scale better with each new participant.
> Secondly, the source is the one that will have a say in who should
> exclusively be granted first access to material, while also ensuring
> that material will be distributed to others in the system after a
> period of exclusive access. Thirdly, we will make use of existing
> resources, experience, manpower etc [to] deal with submissions to
> more efficiently. Fourthly, we will be able to deliver information
> more directly to where it matters and will be used, while remaining
> a neutral service ourselves. And last but not least, this approach will
> create a large union of shared interests in the defense of the rights to
> run an anonymous post-drop in the digital world.[14]

The battle over WikiLeaks has had another salutary effect: it
has delivered a wake-up call to everyone who thought the free
and open Internet was already a fact. Freedom of the press
is no longer the exclusive province of those who own one,
but while the Internet has drastically lowered the barriers
to entry into the public sphere, it has not eliminated them.

Especially when that public sphere is built on privately owned infrastructure.

Take Amazon's hasty decision to kick WikiLeaks off its cloud servers after a mere phone call from a staffer for Senator Joe Lieberman. In its blog post explaining the decision, Amazon says the group was in violation of its terms of service:

> Our terms of service state that "you represent and warrant that you own or otherwise control all of the rights to the content . . . that use of the content you supply does not violate this policy and will not cause injury to any person or entity." It's clear that WikiLeaks doesn't own or otherwise control all the rights to this classified content. Further, it is not credible that the extraordinary volume of 250,000 classified documents that WikiLeaks is publishing could have been carefully redacted in such a way as to ensure that they weren't putting innocent people in jeopardy.[15]

This is pretty specious reasoning. First of all, no one can own copyright on government documents, however they are obtained. So Amazon's first reason is a stake in the heart of any news organization that might use its servers to handle traffic from posting documents that are in the public domain. Second, Amazon is wrong to claim that Wikileaks has failed to redact the documents it is publishing to take care to prevent injury to others; at the time that Amazon cut WikiLeaks off its service, that was certainly the case with the cables, of which only a tiny percentage had been published. Last, it's absurd for Amazon to insist that nothing on its servers put innocent people in jeopardy. Amazon itself stocks and sells all kinds of books that someone can buy and use to learn how to cause injury to others, such as *The Anarchist Cookbook; Zips, Pipes and Pens: Arsenal of Improvised Weapons*; and *The Do-It-Yourself Gunpowder Cookbook.* Of course, those books should be available to readers: the way to combat speech you dislike is with more speech, not less. And when government authorities try to block access to information, the response companies like Amazon, which de facto now host such a large part of the public sphere on their servers, should take is to push back, not cave in.

At the time, Lieberman's communications director, Leslie Phillips, told me that "Senator Lieberman hopes that what has transpired with Amazon will send a message to other companies,"[16] and indeed that message was received. PayPal,[17] Visa, MasterCard, Bank of America, and a small company called Tableau Software all stopped providing services to WikiLeaks in rapid succession. And all of them were acting within their rights as private companies. The First Amendment says "Congress shall make no law . . . abridging the freedom of speech, or of the press," not that private corporations must also embrace free speech. But what happened to WikiLeaks in America shows how easily government can pressure private companies, merely by threatening a criminal investigation of one of their clients and breathing heavily down their necks.

As the editors of the Honolulu Civil Beat, a small nonprofit investigative site, wrote in reaction:

> Alas, the Internet is not free. Nor is it a place of unlimited freedom. We knew that about places like China. But until it became abundantly clear in the WikiLeaks case, not the U.S.A. Sure, it'll be impossible for the government to ever remove what Assange has published from the Internet. This is a case where the cat is definitely out of the bag. But by taking the steps they have to shut down WikiLeaks, governments create a chilling effect on other publishers, making it less likely that information that sheds light on government policy and actions that citizens should know about becomes public.
>
> Consider what the WikiLeaks case might mean for a local publisher. Even a news organization as young as Civil Beat has already received leaked documents from would-be whistle-blowers. We've published articles based on those documents and could very well feel it's the right thing to do to post them on the Internet, as is our practice with many stories.
>
> What would happen if a prosecutor or government official went to the service that was hosting our news service and said we were the subject of a criminal investigation? Civil Beat, like other publishers, relies on payment services provided by a third party, be it PayPal or Visa and MasterCard. Without them, we don't receive revenue. We also depend on third parties to host our website. Yet we've seen in the past week that those ties can easily be severed just by raising the specter of an investigation.[18]

It's worth noting that the publisher of the Civil Beat is Pierre Omidyar, the chairman of eBay, which owns PayPal. (Full disclosure: the Omidyar Network, which he and his wife Pam founded, has given the Sunlight Foundation several million dollars in ongoing support.)

Imagine if your telephone company listened in on your phone calls and cut off the connection if you started talking about WikiLeaks or some other forbidden subject. The analogy isn't perfect, since a one-to-one conversation isn't public in the same way as a blog post with comments. But while there are clear rules preventing telephone service providers from arbitrarily blocking citizens from speaking over the phone lines, there is no such protection for citizens using the Internet. Private telecommunications companies can deny service to a website for the flimsiest of reasons; the same is true for online social networks, which have shut down user accounts or deleted groups with little clear explanation or right of review. There is no right of habeas corpus on Facebook. Not everyone can respond with the resilience of WikiLeaks, which dealt with its situation by spreading to more than one thousand mirror sites in dozens of countries, making it effectively immune from takedown pressure from any one country authority.[19]

Internet users can exert some pressure on these companies to do the right thing, and giants like Google and Twitter have both demonstrated more backbone than did Amazon. In the wake of Amazon's action, Rebecca MacKinnon, a senior fellow at the New America Foundation, wrote an op-ed for CNN reminding us that in 2008, Senator Lieberman tried to get Google to remove videos produced by Islamist terrorist organizations from YouTube. The company took down some that breached its rules against hate speech or promoting violence, but it left many of them up. Eric Schmidt, the company's CEO, told Lieberman, "YouTube encourages free speech and defends everyone's right to express unpopular points of view." He added, "We believe YouTube is a richer and more relevant platform for users precisely because it hosts a diverse range of views, and rather than stifle debate, we allow our users to view all acceptable content and make up their own minds."[20] In the case of WikiLeaks, Schmidt told a conference in Munich that the company had noted the issues raised by serving up WikiLeaks in its search results. His comment was elegant in its simplicity. "Has Google looked at the appropriateness of indexing WikiLeaks? The answer is yes, and we decided to continue," he said. "Because it's legal."[21] More recently, when the U.S. Justice Department demanded that Twitter turn over the records of Assange and four other WikiLeaks activists, the company challenged the secrecy of the order and managed to win the right to alert its users, to give them time to try to challenge the demand in court.

"What are the private sector's obligations and responsibilities to prevent the erosion of democracy?" asks MacKinnon, who is writing a book called *Consent of the Networked* on this very topic. "Given that citizens are increasingly dependent on privately owned spaces for our politics and public discourse . . . the fight over how speech should be governed in a democracy is focused increasingly on questions of how private companies should or shouldn't control speech conducted on and across their networks and platforms."[22]

One answer to this question has come from a loose knit group of online activists who call themselves "Anonymous." It's hard to describe Anonymous, which I suppose is part of the point. Gabriella Coleman, a New York University anthropologist who has studied Anonymous closely, says "there are no leaders, anyone can seemingly join, and participants are spread across the globe, although many of them can be found on any number of Internet Relay Chat Channels where they discuss strategy, plan attacks, crack jokes, and often pose critical commentary on the unfolding events they have just engendered."[23] You might call Anonymous a virtual flash mob, though at times its "members" have gathered physically, as when they organized protests against Scientology in 2008.

In response to anti-WikiLeaks actions by various companies and governmental actors, Anonymous went into action, primarily by directing distributed-denial-of-service (DDOS) attacks at the offending parties websites. These can overload a site's servers and cause it to crash, or otherwise slow down so much as to be inoperable. "Operation Payback" attacked the websites of Amazon, PayPal, MasterCard, Visa, Senator Joe Lieberman, Sarah Palin's political action committee, and the Swiss bank PostFinance, and managed to take down both MasterCard and Visa for about a day, with the other sites suffering shorter outages. The website for the lawyer representing the two Swedish women who have made accusations against Julian Assange was also crashed.[24] MasterCard's and Visa's internal operations were not targeted nor affected; the only people who might have been inconvenienced were customers who might have been trying to go to their websites.

DDOS is a powerful new tool for harassing one's adversaries online, and some political activists have argued that as it doesn't cause any permanent damage, it should be considered a new form of online civil disobedience, like a digital sit-in.[25] However, it's hard to see how you can protest the suppression of online speech by suppressing someone else's online speech. Personally, I agree with cyber-libertarian John Perry Barlow, who called DDOS the "poison gas" of online activism.[26] As a tool, it may do more harm than good, as the kinds of entities that are least able to defend themselves from a concerted denial of service attack tend to be small, independent human rights and dissident groups.[27] They can seek refuge by migrating their services to corporate platforms, like Google's Blogger. But if their goal is to avoid the arbitrary decisions of a private Internet service provider, this is hardly a good outcome. (Law enforcement agencies in the United States, France, Germany, the Netherlands and the United Kingdom have also been searching and in some cases arresting people for allegedly participating in these attacks.[28])

What's needed is much more robust discussion of how the Internet might become a genuinely free public arena, a global town square where anyone can speak. Or, to be more precise, an Internet whose underlying architecture is really free of governmental or corporate control, as decentralized and uncontrollable as life itself. Douglas Rushkoff, an author of many prescient books on the Internet and society, made exactly this point at a symposium Personal Democracy Forum convened on WikiLeaks and Internet freedom in early December 2010. "We don't have the Internet that we think we have—this sort of peer-to-peer, decentralized, uncontrollable, anarchist network." He added, "The net is a great illusion of democracy right now. It is totally top-down controlled and completely centralized."[29]

Alternatives are percolating. As author Evgeny Morozov pointed out in a recent issue of *The New Republic*, "The Cablegate saga has already spurred (or boosted) several nonprofit initiatives that aspire to provide the kind of online services that are essential to a controversial project like WikiLeaks—and do so in a more decentralized and resilient fashion." One, called P2P DNS, was started by a founder of a file-sharing site after the Justice Department and Department of Homeland Security seized eighty-two domain names of sites allegedly selling copyrighted or counterfeit goods. P2P DNS wants to make it impossible for any government to blacklist sites off of the web's domain name system, which is how computers know where to find each other's files.[30] In the long term, these initiatives could enable something like Rushkoff's vision. But for now, unpopular speech online will probably exist in a twilight zone, semi-free, sometimes capable of threatening powerful institutions and other times subject to their whims.

Recently, Sir Tim Berners-Lee, a leading advocate for open government and open data as noted above, was asked his opinion of WikiLeaks and the publication of the Iraq and Afghanistan war logs, as well as Cablegate. He said:

> What happened recently on WikiLeaks was that somebody stole information, somebody had privileged access to information, betrayed the trust put in them in their job, and took information which should not have been, according to their employer, released, and they released it. . . . When we talk about transparency, we're not talking about breaking confidentiality, breaking state secrets or military secrets.[31]

With all due respect for Berners-Lee and his pioneering and ongoing contributions to an open society, he is wrong. Government transparency cannot be defined as only the information that governments deign to share with the public. By his logic—government employees should just do the bidding of their employer—the expense records of the British Parliament would presumably still be secret, or released to the public in such redacted and neutered form as to be of little importance. And the whole political movement in England for greater government transparency of the last two years, which helped propel Berners-Lee into his current position as a top advisor to the British government on open data, might never have come into being.

As President Obama likes to say, "Real change comes from the bottom up."[32] The movement for transparency cannot rely solely on the channels that governments create for addressing requests for public information and greater openness. We have seen how tools like the Freedom of Information Act can be effectively stymied, how individual lawmakers can anonymously block legislation, and how individual bureaucrats can arbitrarily apply or bend rules at their discretion. And we have also seen how government officials frequently and flagrantly leak state secrets when it is to their advantage. A reader of one of Bob Woodward's books will encounter more top secret information supposedly damaging to national security than a visitor to WikiLeaks, yet Woodward is the toast of Washington, while WikiLeaks is deemed a pariah.

Jack Goldsmith, a professor at Harvard Law School and member of the Hoover Institution's Task Force on National Security and Law, served as an assistant attorney general in the Bush administration. It is safe to say he is no fiery radical. He recently noted: "In *Obama's Wars*, Bob Woodward, with the obvious assistance of many top Obama administration officials, disclosed many details about top secret programs, code names, documents, meetings, and the like. I have a hard time squaring the anger the government is directing toward WikiLeaks with its top officials openly violating classification rules and opportunistically revealing without authorization top secret information."[33]

Thus, transparency is also what we can document directly about what our government is doing and who is trying to influence it. If Congress won't track and publish records of which lobbyists are attending what hearings, a journalist or a citizen with a camera can take a snapshot of the people in the room and the public can help flesh out the picture, as NPR did during the health care reform debate.[34] If lobbyists won't say what fundraising parties they are hosting for which politicians, we can get people to leak the invitations and post the data online.[35] And if someone inside government believes they have vital information that would serve the larger public interest by its release, they can leak it. Whistle-blowing is a vital part of a healthy democracy, and also of a health global culture. For people in positions of power, the knowledge that what they are doing might someday be leaked or otherwise exposed can shift behavior in a better direction.

The transparency movement is based on one core idea: that when information about what governments are doing and who is trying to influence them is made broadly available, we as individuals and as a society can better watch over our government, raise questions, root out corruption, highlight problems, elevate solutions, and, in so doing, foster real accountability. At a time when closed and powerful institutions like governments and corporations withhold so much information from us, and have so much information about us, it is vital that ordinary citizens should also have more information about them and what they do. More information, plus the Internet's power to spread it beyond centralized control, is our best defense against opacity and the bad behavior it can enable.

Many of us also believe that improved government transparency is also about more than ferreting out corruption. It can also be the basis for a new kind of participatory and collaborative government, where elected representatives and government agencies work with citizens on identifying problems that need solving, ideas for solving them, and networks for acting together. We envision a day when the boundaries between government and citizens become less rigid and more porous, and elected leaders and other officials shift from being the holders of all power and information and become community conveners, moderators, enablers, and educators. Together, we can gather and share more ideas about what problems need to be addressed and how to solve them than ever before. And instead of expecting government leaders or bureaucrats to solve our problems, we look forward to a day when government acts to enable large numbers of people to connect to each other to better our own lives.

Unfortunately, if we are ever to make real progress toward more open, participatory and accountable government, we have to deal honestly with our sprawling and secretive bureaucracies, not just in the military sector but also including financial agencies and budgetary authorities. Real freedom of speech, including the freedom to connect online, must become the norm worldwide. And we can't profess support for open government, but then turn away from those promises when they prove embarrassing or disruptive to the status quo. Either we believe in the free flow of information, or we do not.

And what that also means for everyone who believes in the power of transparency is that we have to stand up for WikiLeaks' right to publish truthful information, and the right of Internet users everywhere to read it and respond to it. Unpopular speech may be the most difficult speech to protect, but it is also the most valuable speech. And attacks on that freedom are a dagger aimed at the heart of the transparency movement. We should not let them win.

Notes

Chapter 1

1. David Leigh, "Guardian gagged from reporting Parliament," *The Guardian*, October 12, 2009, www.guardian.co.uk/media/2009/oct/12/guardian-gagged-from-reporting-parliament.

2. Guido Fawkes blog, "*Guardian* Gagged From Reporting Parliament," October 12, 2009, http://order-order.com/2009/10/12/guardian-gagged-from-reporting-parliament.

3. Minton report secret injunction gagging *The Guardian* on Trafigura, September 11, 2009, http://mirror.wikileaks.info/wiki/Minton_report_secret_injunction_gagging_The_Guardian_on_Trafigura, 11_Sep_2009.

4. See http://techpresident.com/blog-entry/wikileak-julian-assange-dont-be-martyr for the video of Assange's remarks.

5. Noam Cohen and Brian Stelter, "Iraq Video Brings Notice to a Web Site," The New York *Times*, April 6, 2010, www.nytimes.com/2010/04/07/world/07wikileaks.html, and http://twitter.com/#!/wikileaks/status/7530875613.

6. Kevin Charles Redmon, "WikiLeaks Proves Its Worth as a Backstop," *The Atlantic*, April 6, 2010, www.theatlantic.com/politics/archive/2010/04/wikileaks-provides-its-worth-as-a-backstop/38517.

7. "Exclusive – Julian Assange Extended Interview," *The Colbert Report*, April 12, 2010, www.colbertnation.com/the-colbert-report-videos/260785/april-12-2010/exclusive-julian-assange-extended-interview.

8. Raffi Khatchadourian, "No Secrets: Julian Assange's Mission for Total Transparency," *The New Yorker*, June 7, 2010, www.newyorker.com/reporting/2010/06/07/100607fa_fact_khatchadourian.

9. Ibid.

10. @wikileaks, April 7, 2010, http://twitter.com/#!/wikileaks/status/118016 13697.

11   Noam Cohen, "What Would Ellsberg Do With the Pentagon Papers Today," *The New York Times*, April 19, 2010, www.nytimes.com/2010/04/19/business/media/19link.html.

12   Daniel Ellsberg, *Secrets: A Memoir of Vietnam and the Pentagon Papers* (New York, Penguin, 2002), p. 272.

13   Stephanie Strom, "Pentagon Sees a Threat From Online Muckrakers," *The New York Times*, March 17, 2010, www.nytimes.com/2010/03/18/us/18wiki.html. The Army counterintelligence report, written in 2008, described WikiLeaks as "a potential force protection, counterintelligence, OPSEC and INFOSEC threat to the U.S. Army."

14   Kevin Poulsen and Kim Zetter, "U.S. Intelligence Analyst Arrested in Wikileaks Video Probe," Wired.com, June 6, 2010, www.wired.com/threatlevel/2010/06/leak.

15   Kim Zetter, "Report: U.S. Can't Link Bradley Manning to Julian Assange," Wired.com, January 25, 2011, www.wired.com/threatlevel/2011/01/manning-and-assange.

16   Alissa Rubin, "Two Iraqi Journalists Killed as U.S. Forces Clash With Militias," *The New York Times*, July 13, 2007, www.nytimes.com/2007/07/13/world/middleeast/13iraq.html.

17   Merged Manning-Lamo Chat Logs, http://firedoglake.com/merged-manning-lamo-chat-logs.

18   For more detailed lists of WikiLeaks' impact, see Joshua Norman, "How WikiLeaks Enlightened Us in 2010," CBS News, December 31, 2010, www.cbsnews.com/8301-503543_162-20026591-503543.html; Greg Mitchell, "Why Wikileaks Matters," *The Nation*, January 31, 2011, www.thenation.com/article/157729/why-wikileaks-matters; and "Rainey Reitman," "The Best of Cablegate," Electronic Frontier Foundation, January 7, 2011: www.eff.org/deeplinks/2011/01/cablegate-disclosures-have-furthered-investigative.

19   http://wikileaks.ch/cable/2008/06/08TUNIS679.html. See also https://tunileaks.appspot.com/ for an ongoing compilation of Tunisia-related cables.

20   WikiLeaks' release of the Afghan war documents also raised concerns among leading human rights organizations that they might endanger individuals named in the records who were civilian human rights workers, and the group has so far withheld about 15,000 records to presumably redact the names of such people. Its releases of the Iraq records and State Department cables have so far been conducted in close coordination with

its media partners, who have reportedly sought and received assistance from government authorities concerning what references should be redacted.

21 Ewen MacAskill, "Julian Assange like a hi-tech terrorist, says Joe Biden," *The Guardian*, December 19, 2010, www.guardian.co.uk/media/2010/dec/19/assange-high-tech-terrorist-biden; and Associated Press, "McConnell: WikiLeaks Head a High-Tech Terrorist," December 5, 2010, www.cbsnews.com/stories/2010/12/05/politics/main7119787.shtml.

22 Scott Neuman, "Clinton: WikiLeaks 'Tear at Fabric' of Government," NPR, November 29, 2010, www.npr.org/2010/11/29/131668950/white-house-aims-to-limit-wikileaks-damage.

Chapter 2

1   Micah L. Sifry, "The Rise of Open Source Politics," *The Nation*, November 22, 2004, www.thenation.com/article/rise-open-source-politics.

2   Interview with the author, June 2004.

3   See Fred Turner, *From Counterculture to Cyberculture: Stewart Brand, the Whole Earth Network and the Rise of Digital Utopianism* (University of Chicago Press, 2006).

4   Jay Rosen, "The People Formerly Known as the Audience," PressThink. org, June 27, 2006, http://archive.pressthink.org/2006/06/27/ppl_frmr. html.

5   Howard Rheingold, "Crap Detection 101," SFGate.com, June 30, 2009, www.sfgate.com/cgi-bin/blogs/rheingold/detail?entry_id=42805.

6   Micah L. Sifry, "The Deaning of America," *The Nation*, March 25, 2004, www.thenation.com/article/deaning-america.

7   See Yochai Benkler, *The Wealth of Networks*, (New Haven: Yale University Press, 2006), Chapter Seven: "Political Freedom, Part Two: The Emergence of the Networked Public Sphere," for a detailed exploration of the Diebold case.

Chapter 3

1   See, for example, news-filtering communities like Digg.com, Reditt.com, and Metafilter.com, or specialized hubs like the Internet Movie Data Base (imdb.com).

2   See, for example, @jetblue, @dellcares, @wholefoods, and @comcastcares, for Jet Blue, Dell, Whole Foods, and Comcast's respective social media presences on Twitter.

3   This is, in fact, how the House and Senate currently make the financial disclosure statements of members and their staff, which are required to be public, available.

4   John Robb, "The Tea Party," blog post on Global Guerrillas, February 5, 2010, http://globalguerrillas.typepad.com/globalguerrillas/2010/02/the-tea-party.html.

5   Martin Kaste, "Tea Party Star Leads Movement On Her Own Terms," NPR *Morning Edition*, February 2, 2010, www.npr.org/templates/story/story.php?storyId=123229743.

6   Jonathan Rauch, "How the Tea Party Organizes Without Leaders," *National Journal*, September 11, 2010.

7   The Tea Party Patriots website averages less than 200,000 views a month; its Facebook page boasts 555,000 "likes" and its official Ning site has only 84,000 members as of this writing. *The Washington Post* managed to verify and contact just 647 of the more than 2,500 groups listed on the Tea Party Patriots membership page, and found the typical group size was less than fifty members. See Amy Gardner, "Gauging the scope of the tea party movement in America," *The Washington Post*, October 24, 2010, www.washingtonpost.com/wp-dyn/content/article/2010/10/23/AR2010102304000.html.

8   Pew Internet & American Life Project, "Demographics of Internet Users," May 2010 survey, www.pewinternet.org/Static-Pages/Trend-Data/Whos-Online.aspx.

9   Pew Research Center, "Internet Now Major Source of Campaign News," October 31, 2008, http://pewresearch.org/pubs/1017/Internet-now-major-source-of-campaign-news.

10   Hart/Newhouse MySpace/NBC/*Wall Street Journal* survey, September 2008, http://online.wsj.com/public/resources/documents/poll_findings100108.doc.

11   Liz Gannes, "The Final Online Video Tally: Obama's Long Primary Season Prepped Him for the Win," GigaOM NewTeeVee blog, November 5, 2008, http://gigaom.com/video/the-final-online-video-tally-obamas-long-primary-season-prepped-him-for-the-win.

12   Aaron Smith, "Government Online," Pew Internet & American Life Project," April 27, 2010, www.pewinternet.org/Reports/2010/Government-Online.aspx.

13   Aaron Smith, "The Internet's Role in Campaign 2008," Pew Internet & American Life Project, April 15, 2009, www.pewinternet.org/Press-Releases/2009/The-Internets-Role-in-Campaign-2008.aspx.

14 Aaron Smith, "22% of online Americans used social networking or Twitter for politics, in 2010 campaign," Pew Internet &American Life Project, January 27, 2011, http://pewinternet.org/Reports/2011/Politics-and-social-media.aspx.

15 Andy Bernstein, "Republicans Kicking Democrats' Butt in Social Media," HeadCountBlog, September 23, 2010, www.headcount.org/republicans-kicking-democrats-butt-in-social-media.

16 Pew Global Attitudes Project, "Global Publics Embrace Social Networking," December 15, 2010, http://pewglobal.org/2010/12/15/global-publics-embrace-social-networking.

17 Jennifer Preston, "Movement Began With Outrage and a Facebook Page That Gave It an Outlet," The *New York Times*, February 5, 2011

18 Interview with the author, May 2004.

19 Clay Shirky, transcript of talk at Web 2.0 conference, April 23, 2008, www.herecomeseverybody.org/2008/04/looking-for-the-mouse.html.

Chapter 4

1   David Weinberger, "Transparency is the New Objectivity," JOHO the Blog, July 19, 2009, www.hyperorg.com/blogger/2009/07/19/transparency-is-the-new-objectivity. The video of Weinberger's talk is posted here www.youtube.com/watch?v=o3qSDLF6lU4.

2   John Markoff, "Plan Opens More Data to the Public," The *New York Times*, October 22, 1993.

3   Carl Malamud, "By the People," Address to the Government 2.0 Summit, Washington D.C., September 9, 2009, http://public.resource.org/people.

4   John Markoff, "Group to Widen Access to Federal Data Bases," The *New York Times*, December 23, 1994.

5   Gary Ruskin, "America Off-Line: Gingrich's Unfulfilled Internet Promise," *The Washington Post*, November 16, 1997, www.washingtonpost.com/wp-srv/politics/govt/fedguide/stories/fig112197.htm.

6   Daniel Charles, "2006 Young Innovators Under 35," *Technology Review*, www.technologyreview.biz/TR35/Profile.aspx?TRID=437.

7   Tim O'Reilly, "What Is Web 2.0: Design Patters and Business Models for the Next Generation of Software," O'Reilly Media, September 30, 2005, http://oreilly.com/pub/a/web2/archive/what-is-web-20.html.

8   Ellen Miller, "In the Beginning...," The Sunlight Foundation blog, April 24, 2006, http://sunlightfoundation.com/blog/2006/04/24/in-the-beginning.

9   Dave Green, "The Commons Touch," *The Guardian*, February 13, 2003, www.guardian.co.uk/technology/2003/feb/13/egovernment.politics.

10   Greg Hurst, "The MPs who can't stop talking," *The Sunday Times*, February 27, 2006, www.timesonline.co.uk/tol/news/politics/article735429.ece.

11   Eric Raymond, *The Cathedral and the Bazaar*, www.catb.org/~esr/writings/cathedral-bazaar/cathedral-bazaar/ar01s04.html.

12   Noam Cohen, "Blogger, Sans Pajamas, Rakes Muck and a Prize," *The New York Times*, February 25, 2008, www.nytimes.com/2008/02/25/business/media/25marshall.html.

13   Josh Marshall, Talking Points Memo, May 1, 2006, www.talkingpointsmemo.com/archives/153521.php.

14   Jay Rosen, "They're Not in Your Club, But They Are in Your League: Firedoglake at the Libby Trial," Pressthink.org, March 9, 2007, http://archive.pressthink.org/2007/03/09/libby_fdl.html.

15   Jim Harper, "Help Control Earmarks—And Win an Amazon Kindle," WashingtonWatch.com, July 20, 2009, www.washingtonwatch.com/blog/2009/07/20/earmark-contest.

16   Jim Harper, "Earmarks Contest Update," WashingtonWatch.com, July 25, 2009, www.washingtonwatch.com/blog/2009/07/25/earmarks-contest-update.

17   "Investigate your MP's expenses," *The Guardian*, http://mps-expenses.guardian.co.uk.

18   Micah L. Sifry, "A See-Through Society: How the Web Is Opening Up Our Democracy," *Columbia Journalism Review*, January–February 2009, www.cjr.org/feature/a_seethrough_society.php.

19   Matt Stoller, "End This Fed," Naked Capitalism, December 1, 2010, www.nakedcapitalism.com/2010/12/matt-stoller-end-this-fed.html.

20   Editorial, "The Fed's Bailout Files," *The Wall Street Journal*, December 2, 2010, http://online.wsj.com/article/SB10001424052748704594804575649001391273386.html.

Chapter 5

1   See www.righttoinformation.info for more background.

2   Andrew Heavens, "The web watchdog biting Kenya's MPs," BBC News, March 14, 2007, http://news.bbc.co.u./2/hi/africa/6412143.stm.

3   Ory Okolloh, "Update Jan 3 11:00pm," KenyanPundit, January 3, 2008, www.kenyanpundit.com/2008/01/03/update-jan-3-445-1100-pm.

4   Erik Hersman, "It's Not About Us, It's About Them," WhiteAfrican.com,

January 4, 2008, http://whiteafrican.com/2008/01/04/its-not-about-us-its-about-them.

5 Ory Okolloh, "Update Jan 7," KenyanPundit, January 7, 2008, www.kenyanpundit.com/2008/01/06/update-jan-7.

6 Laura Smith-Spark, "Google Earth Turns Spotlight on Darfur," BBC News, April 11, 2007, http://news.bbc.co.uk/2/hi/africa/6543185.stm. Activists in Bahrain also used Google Earth to show their fellow citizens the palatial landholdings of the ruling family; the juxtaposition of these images against the more cramped residential spaces of working class Bahrainis helped drive turnout in the 2006 elections and swept a number of reformers into Parliament. William Wallis, "Google Earth spurs Bahraini equality drive," *Financial Times*, November 24, 2006.

7 Ory Okolloh, "Ushahidi.com," KenyanPundit, January 9, 2008, www.kenyanpundit.com/2008/01/09/ushahidicom.

8 Erik Hersman, "Ushahidi Updates – SMS, Red Cross, Flickr, etc..." White African.com, January 10, 2008, http://whiteafrican.com/2008 /01/10/ushahidi-updates-sms-red-cross-flickr-etc.

9 See http://katrina05.blogspot.com.

10 Ethan Zuckerman has a comprehensive write up recounting the lessons of the post-Katrina efforts of volunteer coders on his blog, My Heart's in Accra: "Recovery 2.0 – thoughts on what worked and failed on PeopleFinder so far," September 6, 2005, www.ethanzuckerman.com/blog/2005/09/06/recovery-20-thoughts-on-what-worked-and-failed-on-peoplefinder-so-far.

11 Al Tompkins, "NPR's Andy Carvin on the Role of Social Media in Gustav Coverage," Poynter, September 1, 2008, www.poynter.org/latest-news/als-morning-meeting/91234/nprs-andy-carvin-on-the-role-of-social-media-in-gustav-coverage.

12 Nina Keim and Jessica Clark, "Public Media 2.0 Field Report: Building Social Media Infrastructure to Engage Publics," October 2009, Center for Social Media, www.centerforsocialmedia.org/future-public-media/documents/field-reports/public-media-20-field-report-building-social-media-infra. See also Nancy Scola and Allison Fine, "Twitter: An Antidote to Election Day Voting Problems?" October 6, 2008, http://techpresident.com/node/6411.

13 A resulting visualization, http://votereport.us/TimeView/applet/index.html, shows how those reports rolled in across the country, time-stamped and geo-located.

14   Nancy Scola, "Collaborative, Citizen-Driven Election Monitoring Reaches India," techPresident.com, April 6, 2009, http://techpresident.com/blog-entry/collaborative-citizen-driven-election-monitoring-reaches-india.

15   Patrick Meier, "Haiti: Taking Stock of How We Are Doing," February 6, 2010, http://blog.ushahidi.com/index.php/2010/02/06/ushahidi-how-we-are-doing.

16   Andrew Buncombe, "ipaidabribe.com—India's front line in the war on corruption," *The Independent*, October 30, 2010, www.independent.co.uk/news/world/asia/ipaidabribecom-ndash-indias-front-line-in-the-war-on-corruption-2120527.html.

17   Helen Clegg, "Wiki pinpoints Brazilian crime," BBC News, April 15, 2008, http://news.bbc.co.uk/2/hi/7347101.stm.

18   See http://transparency.globalvoicesonline.org.

19   Sowmya Kidambi, "Right to Know; Right to Live: Building a campaign for the right to information and accountability," *New Tactics in Human Rights*, 2008 and author interview in 2011 with Nikhil Dey of the Mazdoor Kisan Shakti Sangathan.

20   From the Eight Principles of Open Government Data, http://resource.org/8_principles.html:

Government data shall be considered open if it is made public in a way that complies with the principles below:

1. Complete: All public data is made available. Public data is data that is not subject to valid privacy, security or privilege limitations.

2. Primary: Data is as collected at the source, with the highest possible level of granularity, not in aggregate or modified forms.

3. Timely: Data is made available as quickly as necessary to preserve the value of the data.

4. Accessible: Data is available to the widest range of users for the widest range of purposes.

5. Machine processable: Data is reasonably structured to allow automated processing.

6. Non-discriminatory: Data is available to anyone, with no requirement of registration.

7. Non-proprietary: Data is available in a format over which no entity has exclusive control.

8. License-free: Data is not subject to any copyright, patent, trademark or trade secret regulation. Reasonable privacy, security and privilege restrictions may be allowed.

21 See CivicCommons.org and Open311.org for more information, and especially their wiki pages.

Chapter 6

1 President Barack Obama, "Transparency and Open Government," January 21, 2009, www.whitehouse.gov/the_press_office/Transparency andOpenGovernment.

2 President Barack Obama, "Freedom of Information Act," January 21, 2009, www.whitehouse.gov/the_press_office/FreedomofInformationAct.

3 William Branigin, "Democrats Take Majority in House; Pelosi Poised to Become Speaker," *The Washington Post*, November 8, 2006, www.washingtonpost.com/wp-dyn/content/article/2006/11/07/AR2006110700473.html.

4 A full list of participants in the Open House Project can be found here: www.theopenhouseproject.com/press/launch.

5 John Wonderlich, "Open House Project Retrospective," The Open House Project, October 14, 2008, www.theopenhouseproject.com/2008/10/14/open-house-project-retrospective. It's also worth noting that press credentialing for citizen journalists and bulk access to congressional floor and committee video were two recommendations that the project made the least progress on.

6 Micah L. Sifry, "Obama as Crowdsourcer; Organizing the Country for Change and Accountability," techPresident.com, February 8, 2009, http://techpresident.com/blog-entry/obama-crowdsourcer-organizing-country-change-and-accountability.

7 Clint Hendler, "Obama on Recovery.gov," *Columbia Journalism Review*, February 9, 2009, www.cjr.org/the_kicker/obama_on_recoverygov.php.

8 Edward Luce and Tom Braithwaite, "US stimulus tsar to unleash 1m inspector-generals," *The Financial Times*, August 20, 2009, www.ft.com/cms/s/0/e731fd52-8db0-11de-93df-00144feabdc0.html#axzz1AZfFLMQT.

9 Earl Devaney, "Chairman's Corner," Recovery.gov, March 22, 2010, www.recovery.gov/News/chairman/Pages/march222010.aspx.

10 Clay Johnson, "Recovery.gov: Stop with the Data Defense, Start with the Conversation," March 30, 2010, http://sunlightlabs.com/blog/2010/recoverygov-stop-data-defense-start-conversation.

11 Earl Devaney, "Chairman's Corner," Recovery.gov, October 27, 2010, www.recovery.gov/News/chairman/Pages/2010Oct27.aspx

12 Becky Hogge, "Open Data Study," Open Society Foundations Information Program, May 2010, www.soros.org/initiatives/information/focus/communication/articles_publications/publications/open-data-study-20100519.

13 Matthew Eric Glassman et al, "Social Networking and Constituent Communications: Member Use of Twitter During a Two-Week Period in the 111th Congress," Congressional Research Service, September 21, 2009, and Matthew Eric Glassman et al, "Social Networking and Constituent Communications: Member Use of Twitter During a Two-Month Period in the 111th Congress," Congressional Research Service , February 3, 2010.

14 Beth Noveck, "Wiki-Government," *Democracy: A Journal of Ideas*, Winter 2008, www.democracyjournal.org/printfriendly.php?ID=6570.

15 Ross Mayfield, "Wiki Deliberation Passes Bill in Legislature," WebProNews, February 7, 2007, www.webpronews.com/blogtalk/2007/02/07/wiki-deliberation-passes-bill-in-legislature.

16 Senator Dick Durbin, "Legislation 2.0: Getting our discussion underway," OpenLeft.com, July 24, 2007, http://openleft.com/showDiary.do? diaryId =363. See also http://archive.redstate.com/stories/congress/senator_durbin_live_at_redstate for his participation on RedState.com.

17 See www.google.com/moderator/#15/e=eea&t=eea.40&f=eea.242c7 for the results.

18 See http://majorityleader.gov/YouCut for details.

19 See http://open.nysenate.gov/legislation/comments.

20 Andrew Hoppin, "Track Public Comments on Legislation with NYSenate 'Bill Buzz'," New York State Senate, December 21, 2010, www.nysenate.gov/blogs/2010/dec/21/track-public-comments-legislation-nysenate-bill-buzz. Full disclosure: Along with Andrew Rasiej, I consulted for the New York State Senate in 2009, offering guidance to its new technology staff on how they could update their operations.

21 Beth Noveck, "Turning Rule Writers into Problem Solvers: Creating a 21st Century Government That's Open and Competent by Improving Regulation and Regulatory Review," Cairns Blog, January 26, 2011, http://cairns.typepad.com/blog/2011/01/turning-rule-writers-into-problem-solvers-creating-a-21st-century-government-thats-open-and-competen.html.

22 Rep. Greg Walden, "The House's Online, Open Transition," Politico, January 5, 2011, www.politico.com/news/stories/0111/47068.html.

23 See http://petitions.number10.gov.uk.

24 Ed Mayo and Tom Steinberg, "The Power of Information," June 2007, http://webarchive.nationalarchives.gov.uk/20100413152047/http://www.cabinetoffice.gov.uk/media/cabinetoffice/corp/assets/publications/reports/power_information/power_information.pdf.

25 Tom Watson, "Power of Information: New Taskforce," March 31, 2008, http://webarchive.nationalarchives.gov.uk/20100413152047/www.cabinetoffice.gov.uk/about_the_cabinet_office/speeches/watson/080331watson.aspx.

26 Micah L. Sifry, "Gov 2.0 Summit: Tom Steinberg on .gov Sites as Public Goods," techPresident, September 9, 2009, http://techpresident.com/blog-entry/gov-20-summit-tom-steinberg-gov-sites-public-goods.

27 Tom Young, "Sir Tim Berners-Lee to help open up government information," *Computing*, June 10, 2009, www.computing.co.uk/ctg/news/1840530/sir-tim-berners-lee-help-government-information.

28 James Crabtree and Tom Chatfield, "Mash the State," *Prospect* magazine, February 2010.

29 Simon Rogers, "Government spending over £25,000: Download the data and help analyse it with our new app," *The Guardian*, November 19, 2010, www.guardian.co.uk/news/datablog/2010/nov/19/government-spending-data.

30 Rebecca Carr, "Public Asked to Shape Open-Government Bill," *Austin American-Statesman*, April 13, 2008.

31 Interview with the author, fall 2008.

32 Lawrence Lessig, "Against Transparency," *The New Republic*, October 9, 2009, www.tnr.com/print/article/books-and-arts/against-transparency.

Chapter 7

1 Remarks by President Barack Obama at Town Hall Meeting with Future Chinese Leaders, Museum of Science and Technology, Shanghai, China, November 16, 2009, www.whitehouse.gov/the-press-office/remarks-president-barack-obama-town-hall-meeting-with-future-chinese-leaders.

2 David Cameron, "The next age of government," TED conference, February 16, 2010, http://blog.ted.com/2010/02/16/the_next_age_of. Transcript from http://dotsub.com/view/0e993622-684f-4e04-93d4-8fcabe1cf5c8/viewTranscript/eng.

3 Gordon Brown, "Wiring a web for global good," TED conference, July 21, 2009, www.ted.com/talks/gordon_brown.html. Transcript from dotsub.com/view/041a25ad-9967-4135-9788-725d9db5c2ab/viewTranscript/eng.

4   "President Obama, Please Get FISA Right," my.barackobama.com/page/
    group/SenatorObama-PleaseVoteAgainstFISA. See also Carlo Scannella,
    "Get FISA Right: Nomadic Democracy," techPresident, July 9, 2008, http://
    techpresident.com/blog-entry/get-fisa-right-nomadic-democracy.
5   Micah L. Sifry, "Fun With YouTube Insight: Who is Watching Obama?"
    techPresident, July 23, 2009, techpresident.com/blog-entry/fun-youtube-
    insight-who-watching-obama. White House blogger Katie Stanton was nice
    enough to give me credit for this observation on the WhiteHouse.gov blog:
    www.whitehouse.gov/blog/2009/07/23/white-house-video-going-global.
6   Bruce Sterling, "The Blast Shack," December 22, 2010, www.webstock.
    org.nz/blog/2010/the-blast-shack.
7   Ed O'Keefe, "OMB: WikiLeaks off-limits to federal workers without
    clearance," *The Washington Post*, December 4, 2010, voices.washington
    post.com/federal-eye/2010/12/wikileaks_off-limits_to_unauth.html; and
    Matt Raymond, "Why the Library of Congress is Blocking WikiLeaks," The
    Library of Congress blog, December 3, 2010, blogs.loc.gov/loc/2010/12/
    why-the-library-of-congress-is-blocking-wikileaks. The public access
    computers were unblocked after a few days.
8   Jacob Lew, "Initial Assessments of Safeguarding and Counterintelligence
    Postures for Classified National Security Information in Automated
    Systems," Memorandum for the Heads of Executive Departments and
    Agencies, M-11-08, Office of Management and Budget, January 3, 2011.
9   Peter Orszag, "Open Government Directive," Memorandum for the Heads
    of Executive Departments and Agencies, M-10-06, Office of Management
    and Budget, December 8, 2009.
10 Heather Brooke, "How I blew up the duck house," *Daily Mail*, March 20,
    2010, www.dailymail.co.uk/news/article-1259445/How-I-blew-duck-
    house-Heather-Brooke-lighting-fuse-biggest-political-scandal-time.
    html.
11 BBC News, "Man behind expenses leak revealed," May 23, 2009, news.
    bbc.co.uk/2/hi/uk_news/politics/8064731.stm.
12 Nik Gowing, "'Skyful of Lies' and Black Swans: The new tyranny of
    shifting information power in crises," Reuters Institute for the Study of
    Journalism, University of Oxford, 2009, www.ox.ac.uk/media/news_
    releases_for_journalists/090511.html.
13 Letters between WikiLeaks and the U.S. government, *The New York Times*,
    http://documents.nytimes.com/letters-between-wikileaks-and-gov.
14 Bill Keller, "Dealing with Julian Assange and the Secrets He Spilled," *The*

New York Times Magazine, January 26, 2011, www.nytimes.com/2011/01/30/magazine/30Wikileaks-t.html.

15 P. J. Crowley, the State Department spokesman, said on January 11, 2011, in a speech to the Washington Center's "Politics and the Media" seminar, "The founder of WikiLeaks has claimed that no one has lost his or her life due to these releases. That is true as far as we know, but that is not the only measure of the impact" (www.state.gov/r/pa/prs/ps/2011/01/154258. htm). Pentagon spokesman Geoff Morell said on August 11, 2010, "We have yet to see any harm come to anyone in Afghanistan that we can directly tie to exposure in the WikiLeaks documents," a statement that was reaffirmed by an unnamed Pentagon official who was interview by Nancy Youssef of McClatchy Newspapers for her November 28, 2010, report, "Officials may be overstating the danger from WikiLeaks," www. mcclatchydc.com/2010/11/28/104404/officials-may-be-overstating-the. html#ixzz1AsY5oCjo.

16 Javier Moreno, "Why *El País chose to publish the leaks," El País, December 23, 2010, www.elpais.com/articulo/english/Why/PAIS/chose/to/publish/the/leaks/elpepueng/20101223elpeng_3/Ten.*

17 David Edwards, "Gingrich: Assange an 'enemy combatant' but fault is Obama's," Raw Story, December 5, 2010, www.rawstory.com/rs/2010/12/gingrich-assange-enemy-combatant

18 Sarah Palin, "Serious Questions about the Obama Administration's Incompetence in the Wikileaks Fiasco," Palin Facebook page, November 29, 2010, www.facebook.com/note.php?note_id=465212788434.

19 Holly Ramer, "Santorum: WikiLeaks chief a terrorist," Associated Press, December 1, 2010, www.concordmonitor.com/article/226759/santorum-wikileaks-chief-terrorist.

20 William Kristol, "Whack WikiLeaks," *The Weekly Standard*, November 30, 2010, www.weeklystandard.com/blogs/whack-wikileaks_520462.html

21 "Fox News' Bob Beckel Calls For 'Ilegally' Killing Assange: 'A Dead Man Can't Leak Stuff' (video)," *The Huffington Post*, December 7, 2010, www.huffing tonpost.com/2010/12/07/fox-news-bob-beckel-calls_n_793467.html.

22 Jennifer Epstein, "Rep. Peter King: Prosecute WikiLeaks, Julian Assange," November 29, 2010, Politico, www.politico.com/news/stories/1110/45667.html.

23 Elisabeth Bumiller, "Gates on Leaks, Wiki and Otherwise," *The New York Times*, November 30, 2010, http://thecaucus.blogs.nytimes.com/2010/11/30/gates-on-leaks-wiki-and-otherwise.

24 Fareed Zakaria, "WikiLeaks Shows the Skills of U.S. Diplomats," *Time*, December 2, 2010, www.time.com/time/world/article/0,8599,2034284, 00.html.

25 Mark Landler, "From WikiLemons, Clinton Tries to Make Lemonade," *The New York Times*, December 4, 2010, www.nytimes.com/2010/12/05/world/05diplo.html.

26 Glenn Greenwald, "Joe Biden v. Joe Biden on WikiLeaks," Salon.com, December 18, 2010, www.salon.com/news/opinion/glenn_greenwald/2010/12/18/wikileaks/index.htm.

27 Mark Hosenball, "U.S. Officials Privately Say WikiLeaks Damage Limited," Reuters, January 18, 2011, www.reuters.com/article/idUSN1816319120110118.

28 P. J. Crowley, "Remarks to the Washington Center's 'Politics and the Media' Seminar Students," as prepared for delivery, U.S. Department of State, January 11, 2011, www.state.gov/r/pa/prs/ps/2011/01/154258.htm.

29 Dianne Feinstein, "Prosecute Assange Under the Espionage Act," *The Wall Street Journal*, December 7, 2010, http://online.wsj.com/article/SB10001424052748703989004576533280626335258.html

30 *The Guardian*'s editor Alan Rusbridger was understandably irritated by the failure of most of the media to accurately describe the Cablegate disclosures. Writing in his introduction to *The Guardian*'s new book on WikiLeaks, he noted, "The extent of the redaction process and the relatively limited extent of publication of actual cables were apparently overlooked by many commentators—including leading American journalists—who spoke disparagingly of a 'willy nilly dump' of mass cables and the consequent danger to life. But, to date, there has been no 'mass dump.' Barely two thousand of the 250,000 cables have been published and, six months after the first publication of the war logs, no one has been able to demonstrate any damage to life or limb." Alan Rusbridger, "WikiLeaks: *The Guardian*'s role in the biggest leak in the history of the world," *The Guardian*, January 28, 2011, www.guardian.co.uk/media/2011/jan/28/wikileaks-julian-assange-alan-rusbridger. See also Matthew L. Schafer, "NPR Fesses Up to WikiLeaks Coverage Blunder; Now It's Everyone Else's Turn," December 28, 2010, http://lippmannwouldroll.com/2010/12/28/npr-fesses-up-to-wikileaks-coverage-blunder-now-its-everyone-elses-turn.

31 Max Frankel, "WikiLeaks: Secrets shared with millions are not secret," Comment is Free, *The Guardian*, December 1, 2010, www.guardian.co.uk/commentisfree/cifamerica/2010/nov/30/wikileaks-secrets-pentagon-papers.

32   See www.fas.org/sgp/news/2010/12/clearances.html for a December 1, 2010, colloquy between Rep. Anna Eshoo of the House Permanent Select Committee on Intelligence and John Fitzpatrick, the director of the ODNI Special Security Center, where Fitzpatrick admits that the government lacks anything better than "a ballpark number."

33   Steven Aftergood, Federation of American Scientists, *Secrecy News*, December 14, 2010, www.fas.org/blog/secrecy/2010/12/how_many_ clearances.html.

34   Dana Priest and William Arkin, "A Hidden World, Growing Beyond Control," *The Washington Post*, July 19, 2010, http://projects.washington post.com/top-secret-america/articles/a-hidden-world-growing-beyond-control/1.

35   Bruce Schneier, "WikiLeaks," December 9, 2010, www.schneier.com/ blog/archives/2010/12/wikileaks_1.html.

36   Summary of Findings and Recommendations, Report of the Commission on Protecting and Reducing Government Secrecy, 1997, www.fas.org/sgp/ library/moynihan/sum.html.

37   Daniel Ellsberg, *Secrets: A Memoir of Vietnam and the Pentagon Papers* (New York, Penguin, 2002), pp. 237–239.

38   Chairman's Foreword, Report of the Commission on Protecting and Reducing Government Secrecy, 1997, www.fas.org/sgp/library/moynihan/ foreword.html.

39   Polly Curtis, "Ministers must 'wise up not clam up' after WikiLeaks disclosures," *The Guardian*, December 30, 2010, www.guardian.co.uk/politics/ 2010/dec/30/wikileaks-freedom-information-ministers-government.

40   Jeff Jarvis, "WikiLeaks, Power shifts from secrecy to transparency," Buzzmachine.com, December 4, 2010, www.buzzmachine.com/2010/ 12/04/wikileaks-power-shifts-from-secrecy-to-transparency.

41   Carne Ross, "WikiLeaks whistle blows time on the old game," *The New Statesman*, December 6, 2010, www.newstatesman.com/society/2010/12/ wikileaks-governments-cables.

42   Interview with Julian Assange, *Paris Match*, January 10, 2011, translated by Mark K. Jensen, http://wlcentral.org/node/876.

43   Paul Kane, "House Staffers Livid Over Website," *The Washington Post*, April 9, 2008, www.washingtonpost.com/wp-dyn/content/article/2008/04/08/ AR2008040803034.html.

44   Clay Shirky, "Half-formed thought on WikiLeaks and global action," Shirky.com, December 31, 2010, www.shirky.com/weblog/2010/12/half-formed-thought-on-wikileaks-global-action.

45 Cory Doctorow, "We Need a Serious Critique of Net Activism," *The Guardian*, January 25, 2011, www.guardian.co.uk/technology/2011/jan/25/net-activism-delusion.

Chapter 8

1   Philip Shenon, "Civil War at WikiLeaks," The Daily Beast, September 3, 2010, www.thedailybeast.com/blogs-and-stories/2010-09-03/wikileaks-organizers-demand-julian-assange-step-aside.

2   Marina Jimenez, "Q&A: Birgitta Jonsdottir on WikiLeaks and Twitter," *The Globe and Mail*, January 12, 2011, www.theglobeandmail.com/news/opinions/qa-birgitta-jonsdottir-on-wikileaks-and-twitter/article1866270.

3   Mark Hosenball, "Is WikiLeaks Too Full of Itself?" *Newsweek*, August 26, 2010, www.newsweek.com/blogs/declassified/2010/08/26/is-wikileaks-too-full-of-itself.print.html.

4   Kevin Poulsen and Kim Zetter, "Unpublished Iraq War Logs Trigger Internal WikiLeaks Revolt," Wired.com, September 27, 2010, www.wired.com/threatlevel/2010/09/wikileaks-revolt.

5   Steven Aftergood, "Wikileaks Fails 'Due Diligence' Review," *Secrecy News*, June 28, 2010, www.fas.org/blog/secrecy/2010/06/wikileaks_review.html.

6   Sarah Ellison, "The Man Who Spilled the Secrets," *Vanity Fair*, February 2011, www.vanityfair.com/politics/features/2011/02/the-guardian-201102.

7   Alan Rusbridger, "WikiLeaks: The Guardian's role in the biggest leak in the history of the world," *The Guardian*, January 28, 2011, www.guardian.co.uk/media/2011/jan/28/wikileaks-julian-assange-alan-rusbridger and Marcel Rosenbach and Holger Stark, "An Inside Look at Difficult Negotiations with Julian Assange," Spiegel Online, January 28, 2011, www.spiegel.de/international/world/0,1518,742163,00.html.

8   "Chinese cyber-dissidents launch WikiLeaks, a site for whistleblowers," Agence France-Presse, January 11, 2007, www.theage.com.au/news/Technology/Chinese-cyberdissidents-launch-WikiLeaks-a-site-forwhistleblowers/2007/01/11/1168105082315.html.

9   Julian Assange, "State and Terrorist Conspiracies," November 10, 2006, and "Conspiracy as Governance," December 3, 2006.

10 http://twitter.com/#!/wikileaks/status/9697336829677568.

11 Mark Pesce, "The Blueprint," *The Human Network*, December 5, 2010, http://blog.futurestreetconsulting.com/?p=446.

12 Mark Hosenball, "The Next Generation of WikiLeaks," Reuters,

January 28, 2011, www.reuters.com/article/2011/01/28/us-wikileaks-idUSTRE70R5A120110128?pageNumber=1.

13 See http://about.lob.by/localeaks/ for details.

14 Micah L. Sifry, "From WikiLeaks to OpenLeaks, Via the Knight News Challenge," techPresident, December 17, 2010, http://techpresident.com/blog-entry/wikileaks-openleaks-knight-news-challenge.

15 Amazon Web Services, http://aws.amazon.com/message/65348.

16 Interview with author, December 1, 2010.

17 PayPal's vice president of platform, Osama Bedier, said that the company acted in response to the State Department legal advisor's letter to WikiLeaks, which declared its receipt of the leaked cables to be a violation of the law. PayPal's terms of service says its payment system "cannot be used for any activities that encourage, promote, facilitate or instruct others to engage in illegal activity." Thus, even though no judicial authority has indicted or convicted WikiLeaks for a crime, PayPal deemed the State Department's letter sufficient proof of illegality. See www.thepaypalblog.com/2010/12/paypal-statement-regarding-wikileaks/ and http://techcrunch.com/2010/12/08/paypal-wikileaks.

18 Editorial board, "Internet Press Vulnerable After WikiLeaks," *Honolulu Civil Beat*, December 9, 2010, www.civilbeat.com/posts/2010/12/09/7276-internet-press-vulnerable-after-wikileaks.

19 James Cowie, "WikiLeaks: Moving Target," Renesys blog, December 7, 2010, www.renesys.com/blog/2010/12/wikileaks-moving-target.shtml.

20 Rebecca MacKinnon, "WikiLeaks, Amazon and the new threat to Internet speech," December 2, 2010, http://articles.cnn.com/2010-12-02/opinion/mackinnon.wikileaks.amazon_1_wikileaks-founder-julian-assange-lieberman-youtube.

21 Reuters, "Eric Schmidt Expects Another 10 Years at Google," January 26, 2011, www.mb.com.ph/articles/300691/eric-schmidt-expects-another-10-years-google.

22 MacKinnon Ibid.

23 Gabriella Coleman, "What It's Like to Participate in Anonymous' Actions," *The Atlantic*, December 20, 2010, www.theatlantic.com/technology/archive/2010/12/what-its-like-to-participate-in-anonymous-actions/67860.

24 Cassell Bryan-Low and Sven Grundberg, "Hackers Rise for WikiLeaks," *The Wall Street Journal*, December 8, 2010, http://online.wsj.com/article/SB10001424052748703493504576007182352309942.html.

25 See Deanna Zandt, "Legitimate civil disobedience: WikiLeaks and the layers of backlash," December 12, 2010, www.deannazandt.com/2010/12/12/legitimate-civil-disobedience-wikileaks-and-the-layers-of-backlash.

26 Peter Apps, "Analysis: WikiLeaks battle a new amateur face of cyber war?" Reuters, December 9, 2010, www.reuters.com/article/idUSTRE6B86OO20101210.

27 See Ethan Zuckerman et al's "2010 Report on Distributed Denial of Service (DDOS) Attacks," Berkman Center for Internet & Society, December 20, 2010, http://cyber.law.harvard.edu/publications/2010/DDoS_Independent_Media_Human_Rights.

28 Press Release: "Search Warrants Executed in the United States as Part of Ongoing Cyber Investigation," Federal Bureau of Investigation, Washington D.C., January 27, 2011, http://www.fbi.gov/news/pressrel/press-releases/warrants_012711.

29 "WikiLeaks and Internet Freedom," Personal Democracy Forum, December 11, 2010, http://personaldemocracy.com/pdfleaks. See also Douglas Rushkoff, "The Next Net," Shareable, January 3, 2011, http://shareable.net/blog/the-next-net.

30 Evgeny Morozov, "Wiki Rehab," *The New Republic*, January 7, 2011, www.tnr.com/print/article/politics/81017/wikileaks-internet-pirate-party-save. See also Project IDONS, http://lauren.vortex.com/archive/000787.html.

31 Alex Howard, "Time Berners-Lee Says WikiLeaks is Not Open Government Data," Huffington Post, December 21, 2010, www.huffingtonpost.com/alexander-howard/tim-bernerslee-on-wikilea_b_798671.html.

32 Actually, both George W. Bush and Barack Obama have used this phrase, though it is much better known as Obama's. See Ann McFeatthers, "Governors split on taxes, back eased federal rules," *Toledo Blade*, February 27, 2001, for an early Bush usage. See Brian Stelter, "The Facebooker Who Friended Obama," *The New York Times*, July 7, 2008, www.nytimes.com/2008/07/07/technology/07hughes.html for an early Obama usage.

33 Jack Goldsmith, "Seven Thoughts About WikiLeaks," Lawfare, December 10, 2010, www.lawfareblog.com/2010/12/seven-thoughts-on-wikileaks.

34 "Turning the Camera Around: Health Care Stakeholders," NPR, www.npr.org/news/specials/2009/hearing-pano.

35 See the Sunlight Foundation's www.PoliticalPartyTime.org.

Resource Guide

What follows is a highly selective list of organizations working on the issues of government transparency, Internet freedom and we-government.

U.S.-based:
— **Personal Democracy Forum** (PersonalDemocracy.com). The world's leading gathering place for everyone interested in how technology is changing politics, government and civil society. Since 2004, PdF has hosted an annual conference in New York City, and more recently added satellite conferences in Europe and Latin America. In addition, PdF publishes the award-winning techPresident.com blog, which covers this changing world on a daily basis, and produces regular salons, conference calls, and professional guides for members of the PdF Network community.

The **Sunlight Foundation** (SunlightFoundation.com). A non-profit organization that uses cutting-edge technology and ideas to make government more transparent and accountable. Founded in 2006, Sunlight develops new policies to open government; builds tools and websites to enable easy access to information; engages in advocacy for twenty-first century laws to require that government make data available in real time; and trains thousands of journalists and citizens to better watchdog politics in the United States. See also its directory of "Insanely Useful Websites" at SunlightFoundation.com/resources.

— **Open Congress** (OpenCongress.org). A joint project of the Participatory Politics Foundation and the Sunlight Foundation that brings together official government data with news and blog coverage, social networking, and public participation tools, all in a user-friendly fashion. It is also a resource for in-depth information on government transparency projects (see its "Third Party Websites That Transform Government Data" wiki page for more information: OpenCongress.org/wiki/Third_Party_Websites_That_Transform_Government_Data).

— The **Electronic Frontier Foundation** (EFF.org). Founded in 1990, EFF is an international non-profit digital rights advocacy and legal organization based in the United States. Blending the expertise of lawyers, policy analysts, activists, and technologists, it is the leading organization defending individual civil liberties online.

— **Public.Resource.org**. A non-profit organization dedicated to publishing and sharing public domain materials in the United States whose motto is "Making Government Information More Accessible."

— **Civic Commons** (CivicCommons.org). A new nonprofit organization that works to help entities at all levels of government share code and best practices, reform procurement practices, and learn to function not only as a provider of services but as a platform to which an ecosystem of industry can add value for government and its citizens.

International:
— The **Technology for Transparency Network** (transparency.globalvoicesonline.org). A research and mapping project that aims to improve understanding of the current state of online technology projects that increase transparency and accountability in countries around the world. The project is supported by the Transparency and Accountability Initiative, a donor collaborative that includes the Ford Foundation, Hivos, the International Budget Partnership, the Omidyar Network, the Open Society Institute, the Revenue Watch Institute, the United Kingdom Department for International Development (DFID) and the William and Flora Hewlett Foundation.

— The **Global Network Initiative** (GlobalNetworkInitiative.org). A non-governmental organization founded in 2008 that works to prevent Internet censorship by authoritarian governments and protect the Internet privacy rights of individuals. It is sponsored by a coalition of multinational corporations, non-profit organizations and universities, including Google, Microsoft, Yahoo!, Human Rights Watch, the Berkman Center for Internet & Society, the Center for Democracy and Technology, and the Electronic Frontier Foundation.

— **Wikipedia's "Parliamentary Informatics"** page (wikimedia.org/ wikipedia/en/wiki/Parliamentary_informatics) offers a detailed list of country-by-country and international hubs for online information for the documentation of legislative activity. Worth noting: France's NosDeputes.fr, Germany's

Parliament Watch (AbgeordnetenWatch.de), Ireland's KildareStreet. com, Israel's OpenKnesset (oknesset.org), Italy's OpenParlamento (parlamento.openpolis.it), Kenya's Mzalendo.com, Open New Zealand (open.org.nz) and UNDemocracy.org, which covers the United Nations.

— **mySociety** (mySociety.org). An e-democracy project of the UK Citizens Online Democracy charity, founded in 2003, that runs most of the best-known democracy and transparency websites in the United Kingdom, including TheyWorkForYou.com, WriteToThem.com and FixMyStreet.com. It also built the 10 Downing Street Petitions Website for the Prime Minister's Office, and has spawned sister efforts in Australia (OpenAustralia.org) and New Zealand (TheyWorkForYou.co.nz).

— **Ushahidi** (Ushahidi.com). A non-profit tech company based in Kenya that specializes in developing free and open source software for information collection, visualization and interactive mapping and builds tools for democratizing information, increasing transparency and lowering the barriers for individuals to share their stories. Its team of paid and volunteer developers are based primarily in Africa, but also Europe, South America and the U.S.

— **Vota Intelligente** (VotaInteligente.cl). A project of the Fundación Ciudadano Inteligente ("Smart Citizen Foundation"), a Chilean-based non-governmental organization that promotes transparency and accountability in Latin American politics by collecting data and delivering it to citizens through the web and the use of web applications. See also Brazil's Congresso Aberto (CongressoAberto.com.br), and Colombia's Congreso Visible (CongresoVisible.org)

— The **Philippine Public Transparency Reporting Project** (TransparencyReporting.net). A collaboration of four media development organizations—the Institute for War and Peace Reporting (IWPR), the Center for Community Journalism and Development (CCJD), the Mindanao News and Information Cooperative Center (MindaNews) and the National Union of Journalists of the Philippines (NUJP)—that work alongside and through existing and new media to monitor, mobilize and demand greater public transparency and accountability.

— **Visible Government** (VisibleGovernment.ca). A Canadian non-profit organization that promotes online tools for government transparency, tracks government data disclosure, and advocates for improvements in government policy.

— **La Quadrature du Net** (LaQuadrature.net). A French advocacy group that promotes the rights and freedoms of citizens on the Internet. More specifically, it advocates for the adoption of French and European legislation to respect the founding principles of the Internet, most notably the free circulation of knowledge. To that aim, La Quadrature du Net engages in public-policy debates concerning freedom of speech, copyright, regulation of telecommunications and online privacy.

— The **Chaos Computer Club** (CCC.de). An organization of hackers based in Germany and other German-speaking countries that strives for more transparency in government, freedom of information, and human right to communication. Founded in Berlin in 1981, it also fights for free access to computers and technological infrastructure for everybody. See also the Open Data Network (opendata-network.org).

— **EU Transparency** (EUTransparency.org). A non-profit organization that mixes journalism, data and the web to shed light on how European Union institutions and policies are working. Its main projects are FarmSubsidy.org and FishSubsidy.org, which document government payments to farmers, fishers, and others working in those industries across Europe. See also **VoteWatch.eu**, which collects and displays the full records of the European Parliament.

WikiLeaks resources:
— **WikiLeaks** (WikiLeaks.ch). A non-profit media organization dedicated to bringing important news and information to the public that provides an innovative, secure and anonymous way for independent sources around the world to leak information to our journalists. A list of mirror sites can be found at WikiLeaks.info.

— **WikiLeaks Central** (WLCentral.org). A hub for news, analysis and action run by volunteers supportive of WikiLeaks that covers censorship and freedom of information topics in all forms.

— The **Bradley Manning Support Network** (BradleyManning.org). An ad hoc, international grassroots effort to help accused whistle blower Pfc. Bradley Manning. See also the blog FireDogLake's ongoing coverage (FireDogLake.com/bradley-manning-coverage).